IMAM AL-RABBANI

IMAM AL-RABBANI

Reviver of the Second Millenium

OSMAN NURI TOPBAS
Omer Siddique

Dhikr.

CONTENTS

	Imam Rabbani: Reviver Of The Second Millenium	1
1	The Life of Imam al Rabbani: Ahmed Al-Farooqi Al-Sirhindi 1564 - 1624 C.E.	10
2	Wisdoms from Imam Rabbani - Part 1	60
3	Wisdoms from Imam Rabbani - Part 2	78
4	Wisdoms from Imam Rabbani - Part 3	96
5	Wisdoms from Imam Rabbani - Part 4	113
6	Wisdoms from Imam Rabbani - Part 5	130
7	Wisdoms from Imam Rabbani - Part 6	143
8	Wisdoms from Imam Rabbani - Part 7	159

Imam Rabbani: Reviver of the Second Millenium

Author's Introduction

In the Name of Allah, Most Gracious, Most Merciful,

All praises are to Allah (swt), who honoured us with the blessing of Islam and faith and elevated us to be the addressees of His Exemplary Speech through the Noble Quran. And that He made us from the nation of the Prophet of guidance and instruction, our master, Muhammad, upon him be prayers of peace – who himself was a living and walking explanation of the Great Quran.

So prayers and peace be upon our leader, our standard of what is right in this world, our intercessor in the next world, the pride of all creation, our master, Muhammad, who was sent as a mercy to the worlds and upon his family, and his companions – those pure and holy ones...

Truly, those elevated personalities who are taken as examples and models after the Prophet (s) and his noble companions, are the scholars and those with deep knowledge. They are considered as the inheritors of the Prophet (s) because of their knowledge, deep understandings of reality and exemplary conduct.

The 'People of Allah' are believing scholars and those with deep inner knowledge and the truthful ones who carry the responsibilities of the *ummah* (nation of believers). They:

- Are those who have successfully joined the outer aspects of religion with the inner ones, while adhering to the principles and laws of Islam.
- Are those who have traversed and surpassed the levels of the heart by turning their backs to the deception of this world, and by focusing on piety and righteousness have reached the pinnacles of good conduct and righteous deeds.
- Are those that strive diligently to rid humanity from unsavoury and evil characteristics and from the desires and lusts of the ego-centric self (*nafs*) and help mankind to arrive at praiseworthy characteristics and spiritual completeness.

Allah (swt) mentions in His Noble Book:

'O believers! Be mindful of Allah and be with the truthful.'[1]

The *Shaykh, Khawja Abeedullah Ahrar* says in explaining this verse:

*'The command that appears here in this verse – **be with the truthful** – expresses a meaning of accompanying the truthful ones continuously. The unconditional mention here of companionship indicates two meanings.*

One being the actual action of physical companionship and the other holding a more abstract meaning. The real companionship is being physically present in the gatherings of the truthful with presence of one's heart. As for the more abstract meaning, it is to imagine their (the truthful ones') spiritual states and to take them as an example and model even in their absences. And recalling their advices and sermons, so full of wisdoms and lessons'

This, then points to how the first step in transforming one's self into a righteous human being, is companionship of the righteous ones and extending the bonds of friendship and love to them. This change of righteousness is a natural result of continual accompanying of the righteous together with feelings of love.

This book is a humble effort on our part and limited by our capability to accompany and be in the presence of one of the truthful (*siddiqeen*) and righteous servants of Allah (swt) – *Imam Rabbani, Ahmed al-Sirhindi* – even if it is in his absence and only an abstract and imaginative association.

Allah (swt) mentions in *Surah Maryam*:

'As for those who believe and do good, the Most Compassionate will (certainly) bless them with (genuine) love.'[2]

So, Allah (swt) honours the servants which He loves with the strange effect of love, that is similar to a magnet, attracting towards it every heart that is lucky enough to have a portion from the treasures of this secret.

Indeed, every human enters this world, which resembles a hotel or inn, as a traveller, staying here for some time before passing on. After some time though, all of one's traces are wiped away from this world until even his name is no longer remembered. Except that Allah (swt) may exclude from such a fate, His beloved ones and His people, so that their remembrance may remain amongst people.

The *awliya* (friends) of Allah (swt) don't simply become part of the past to be thrown into the darkness of forgottenness – not even after their temporal bodies have corroded away. How many from the 'people of truth' are there, whose services to mankind and the traces of their deeds are still among us while they are in the world of the grave (*barzakh*), their works still guiding us and illuminating our paths. And they will certainly remain alive in hearts even after we have passed away. Their lives of guidance have surpassed time, ages and countries due to their closeness with Allah (swt).

If we desire further consideration of this matter and the extent of its reality, then we need not look further at the number of visitors to the graves and shrines of the great ones from the *awliya* – a sufficient proof in this regard.

Additionally, the following incident is a strong evidence and example of the love Allah (swt) propagates among hearts towards his *awliya*:

It has been narrated that the *Abbasid* caliph, *Haroun al-Rashid*, would from time to time, stay in the city of Raqqa, within his vast, sprawling kingdom. Once, one of the great, righteous *awliya*, *Abdullah ibn Mubarak* (r), arrived in Raqqa while the caliph was also there. When *Abdullah ibn Mubarak* (r) was close to entering, the people celebrated and left to meet him en masse, crowding around him in large numbers till the city was practically empty except for the caliph, some of his men and family. One of the caliph's slave-girls looked down from his castle and said, "What happened to the people?"

It was said to her, 'A man from the scholars of *Khurasan* has arrived called *Abdullah ibn Mubarak* and the people have rushed forward to meet him.'

She replied, 'This is true kingdom! Not the kingdom of *Haroun al-Rashid*! Since in the kingdom of *Haroun al-Rashid* not even the workers gather for him if not forced by the guards to do so!'

In actuality, this is true kingdom as material sovereignty and kingdom shall pass away and finish, without fail, someday. As for the authority and kingdom of the heart, it continues and carries on with its same momentum and intensity, even after death. Humanity feels a continuous need for those kings and sultans of the heart and seeks them out in every place to walk in their bright, illuminated footsteps.

There exists astounding and unusual feelings of attachment and affection with the people of truth, despite there passing long centuries since their deaths. Such as Shaykh *Bahaudeen al-Naqshabandi (r), Abdul Qadir al-Jilani (r), Yunus Emre (r), Mawlana Jalaludeen al-Rumi (r), Azeez Mahmoud Hidaai* (r) and many others.

Allah (swt) has persisted the memory of such great scholars who offered valuable services to Islam and its people, like the great *muhaditheen* (scholars of *Hadith*), *mufassireen* (scholars of Quranic exegesis), scholars of the schools of law (*fiqh*) and the people of spiritual purification (*tassawuf* or Sufism).

And no doubt, that one of the kings and spiritual sultans who sits on the throne of the hearts of believers, remaining alive therein, is *Imam Rabbani (Ahmed al-Sirhindi)*.

The result of the exemplary life that this honourable Shaykh spent, who was born in the town of Sirhind, *al-Hind* (present-day India) nearly four and a half centuries ago, in the struggle and protection of *tawheed* (creed of God's Oneness), was that he became so beloved and highly appreciated in the hearts of all Muslims that his love surpassed the borders of India, and in a short while, spread to the rest of the world and continues to do so in our age, today.

Many of the *tariqaat* of *tassawuf* (paths of Sufism), and foremost the *Naqshabandi Tariqa*, rely on the wisdoms of Imam Rabbani (r) and sip from the spring of his spiritual radiance. For he is considered a great guide and a reference and true and practical standard for the nation of Muhammad (s), even after the passing of his temporal, material life. Truly, he has continued to be, from since the time he entered the world of the grave until our present day, a shining beacon of guidance and steadfastness in the service of the religion and in guiding others – and will continue to be so in the future.

It appears in a noble hadith – '*A person is with whom he loves*'. So, if we feel love towards the *awliya*, who are beloved to Allah (swt), and our wish is to be resurrected alongside them on the Day of Resurrection, then we should strive to the level of our capabilities to attain some portion of their faith, their good characters and their steadfastness. Since, from the signs of true love is being adorned with and imitating the state of the beloved.

We should also continually compare our spiritual states (*haal*) against the states of the people of truth, taking them as a standard and true guide and sipping from the springs and fountains of their hearts.

Dearest Readers,

We have desired through this booklet, which forms a part of our series published under the title – *Wisdoms from the Awliya of Allah* – to undertake a meditative journey of the wisdom hidden in the hearts of the people of truth.

Let us not forget that we today are the children and students and companions of the people of truth who have left this temporal world for the everlasting realm, who rightly directed the world, through their exhortations and guidance, such as *Baha ud-Deen Naqshabandi (r), Abdul Qadir al-Jilani (r), Mawlana Jalaluddin al-Rumi (r), Yunus Emre (r), Hidaai (r) and Imam Rabbani al-Sirhindi (r)*. Our wish, and what we seek from Allah (swt) is that He make for us on this earth, when we are in our graves waiting for the Day of Judgement after leaving this temporal world, that He make for us too companions that would remember us with love and goodness that would send us joy and happiness in our souls. Indeed, that is truly a great happiness, that one succeeds in leaving positive echoes and impacts behind for the benefit of the generations to come tomorrow...

We ask Allah (swt) that He give us success in this world in walking on the path of His beloved ones, to perform righteous deeds that would earn His Good-Pleasure and that He gathers us together in the Hereafter with His servants which He loves and is well pleased with.

Ameen![3]

Osman Nuri Topbas

November, 2015

Üsküdar, Istanbul

Footnotes

1. Quran; 9:119
2. Quran; 19:96
3. I would also like to direct my gratitude to Sayyid Muhammad Akif Kunayi who worked very hard in the preparation of this booklet, I ask Allah (swt) that He make his efforts into a continuing charity in the pages of his deeds.

CHAPTER 1

The Life of Imam al Rabbani: Ahmed Al-Farooqi Al-Sirhindi 1564 - 1624 C.E.

Imam Ahmed Sirhindi (also known as Imam Rabbani – r) was born in the town of *Sirhind*, in the jurisdiction of *Al-Hind* (present day India), in the month of *Shawwal*, year 971 of the *hijri* calendar. He was given the title '*Al-Farooqi*' because his lineage returned to our master, *Umar ibn al-Khattab (r)*.

His father, *Al-Sayyid Abdul-Ahad* was gifted with elevated kindness and good-nature. A man of knowledge and *urfaan*[1], and was a bridge between the *Chistiyya* and *Qadiriyya* Sufi lineages, perfecting their outer and inner aspects.

*Imam Ahmed Sirhindi (*r*)* began his education with the memorisation of the Noble Quran, completing it in a short period of time. He received most of his knowledge from his father as well as from the notable scholars in his reach. After obtaining various sciences from his father and the surrounding scholars, he headed towards Sialkot (present-day Pakistan), which was considered a great centre for knowledge and learning. Here, he acquired both religious and other sciences at the hands of various scholars and applied his interest predominantly in the sciences of *Tafseer, Hadith and Fiqh*.

When the Imam reached seventeen years of age, he had already taken great strides in acquiring the external sciences and so returned to his father and began to deliver lessons by his side. In this time, he received license to teach (*ijaza)* in *Tafseer* and *Hadith* from the judge *Bahlool Badakhsani*.

On reaching about 20 years of age, he authored a book he named "*Isaabatul Nabuwa*" (The Target of Prophethood) with which he challenged the heedless scholars of the political establishment of the time, who were deviating towards error, who openly revealed their deep admiration towards Philosophy, as if appointing it to a higher level of authority than prophetic, revealed knowledge. In it he gave both philosophical and traditional evidences that proved the importance of Prophethood and its necessity. He authored other books as well in this period.

After some time, he attached himself with his father and began to continually attend his gatherings, concentrating with determination on spiritual (*tassawuf-focused*) education and training. In order to be persistent in his father's service and devotion, he resolutely accompanied his father and never left him. His father, *Abdul Ahad*, passed away in the year 1007 *Hijri* /1599 *C.E.* A short time before his death, he gave the banner of *khilafah*[2] to his son, *Imam Rabbani, Ahmed Farooqi*.

The following year, 1008 *H*, after his father death and having reached the age of thirty-seven years, *Imam Rabbani* (r) left his hometown of Sirhind in the month of *Rabee-ul-Akhir*[3] and set out for the honoured city of Mecca to fulfil the obligation of *Hajj*[4]. However, once he reached Delhi, he visited the prominent Shaykh, *Al-Baqi billah* (r), on the advice of one his companions and after attending the Shaykh's circle for a period of time, he affiliated and remained with the Shaykh.

Imam Rabbani (r) remained with Shaykh *Al-Baqi billah* (r) for a period approaching three months. He was then obliged to return home as the season of *Hajj* had passed him by. Through correspondence of letters, his *Shaykh (Al-Baqi billah)*, was aware of the young Imam's spiritual states and his progression and it wasn't long before *Imam Rabbani* (r) visited his teacher for a second time. It was in this visit he was given *ijaza* or license to teach *tassawuf* (Sufism or purification of the self). After spending another couple of months in the shade of his Shaykh, the Imam returned home, now beginning to guide the people in accordance with the etiquette of the *Naqshbandi Tariqa* (as learnt from his shaykh). He perceived, at this time, a spiritual deficiency in himself, and thought about retiring from teaching so he could seclude himself in isolation. Such thoughts may have gotten the better of him if not for the persistence of his students which pushed him to carry on with the guidance and reformation of the people.

On his third visit to Shaykh *al-Baqi billah* (r), he chanced upon his Shaykh on the way. The Shaykh thus showed his consideration and a great welcoming for him and handed over to him the task of instructing many of his own students!

Even though *Imam Rabbani* (r) had acquired many elevated spiritual states and sublime favours, he would act in front of his shaykh with the utmost discipline, conduct and humility. Once, the shaykh sent one of his students to request the presence of the *Imam Rabbani* (r). Upon hearing his teacher's summons, *Imam Rabbani* (r) immediately turned pale and began quivering as if in deep fear and panic. His teacher would reciprocate this high esteem, showing towards him utmost honour and love.

After the passing away of Shaykh *al-Baqi billah* (r), Imam Rabbani (r) continued with his teaching and guiding in Sirhind and began corresponding by letters to his students living in far-off townships as well as to men of political authority. To his students, his letters outlined some of the finer points of *tassawuf*. As for those directed to the leaders, they focused more on the foundations and essentials of Islam and general issues associated with the proper way of the people of *ahl ul-Sunnah wal-Jama'ah*[5].

Imam Rabbani (r) would remember the passing of his shaykh every year in the month of his passing – *Jumad-ul-akhir* – by visiting his graveside before returning home to Sirhind.

HIS RELATIONSHIP WITH THE SULTANS

Sultan Babur Akbar Shah initially was a righteous Muslim holding an *aqeedah*[6] which was orthodox, pure and sound. He was unlettered, not knowing reading nor writing, being prevented from knowledge and learning because of political circumstances and the numerous upheavals induced by them. Later, he deviated towards unorthodox and misguided ideas under the influence of the scholars surrounding him whose primary motive was the acquisition of material, worldly interests. These men of knowledge aimed for status with the sultans and other men of authority and would exert their efforts to appear charming and acceptable before them. They were to blame for the agitation and awakening of many doubts and suspicions against Islam and the wealthy where especially misled by the stirring up of contentious issues and fixation upon them.[7]

As a result, Sultan Akbar Shah, losing his religious integrity, bestowed important administrative roles to non-Muslims and allowed Hindu women into his harem. He proceeded to encourage his right-hand men on creating a new religion called *Al-Deen-i-Ihahi* (The Divine Religion) with the claim of uniting between Islam and Hinduism. *Masaajid* in some places where demolished to build Hindu temples in their places.

He also issued forth a command obliging people to prostrate before him as a gesture of honour and reverence towards him. Although this was of no importance amongst the Hindus, it presented a great and serious problem to sincere, honest Muslims. Those who followed their base desires, chasing material benefits as well as ignorant and corrupted scholars who desired the good-will and love of the sultan issued forth *fatawah*[8] proclaiming the legality of prostrating before the sultan justifying it on the grounds that the prostration was with the intention of salutation and respect and not with the intention of worship.

Imam Rabbani (r) proceeded to the capital Agra and met some of those intimate with the sultan and said to them, '*The sultan has found himself in defiance of Allah(swt) and His Messenger (s). Remind him that his kingdom and sovereignty will soon end (like all worldly kingdoms). Let him repent from his sins and return to the straight path of Allah(swt) and His Messenger(s)!*'

Some of those who worked in high and prominent positions displayed great respect for *Imam Rabbani* (r) and tried to return the sultan to the straight path. However, the Sultan was submerged in the waves of the new religion he had founded and paid no attention to the advice put forth by these men. Suddenly, the astrologers of Akbar Shah began predicting the coming collapse of his rule and kingdom, causing great anxiety to the sultan, further, the sultan saw strange dreams in those days. This all pushed him to issue the following edict:

"*Whomsoever wishes to embrace Islam, let him do so. And whomsoever wishes to embrace Deen-i-Ilahi, let him do so. There is no force or compulsion for anyone to embrace what they don't want to.*"

On one of the days of festivities, a tent was erected for the followers of the new Deen-i-Ilahi, and another for the followers of Islam. The tent of the people of Deen-i-Ilahi was fashioned with the most splendid and beautiful of fabrics, wherein were tables of the most wholesome and delicious types of food, drink and fruit. As for the tent of the Muslims, it was humble and simple in its fabric and food and even appeared in a state of deficiency and poverty.

Imam Rabbani (r) came to the tent of the Muslims with his followers and they lodged inside. The Imam took a handful of dirt in his hand and threw it in the direction of the tent of the supporters of Deen-i-ilahi. Later, a violent wind raged in the direction of that tent and Akbar Shah and his supporters were left dealing with a difficult situation. All the while, the tent of the Muslims remained tranquil and calm, not having to deal with the like of what had afflicted the other camp. Before these divine and obvious warnings, some of the staff and officers of the state withdrew from their positions and became followers of *Imam Rabbani* (r).

Akbar died in the year 1605 C.E and his son Jehangir inherited the throne after him. This pleased the Imam greatly as he knew Jehangir as a man adhering to Islam.

The Imam sent many of his students as his representatives to various locations for the purpose of spreading guidance and religious instruction. For example, he sent his disciple, *Mir Muhammad Nomani*, to the city of Deccan after giving him license to teach (*khilafa*). Hundreds would frequent him in the lodge (*tekke*[9]) he established where they would busy themselves with the remembrance and contemplation of Allah(swt) and acquirement of knowledge. He also gave license to Shaykh

Badee-ul-deen Sahranpuri and dispatched him first to his own hometown and then to Agra. Likewise, multitudes of men joined circles of remembrance of Allah(swt) and guidance and thousands of officers from the army repented and reformed at the very hands of Imam Rabbani (r).

He also sent seventy people headed by *Maulana Muhammad Qasim* to the area of Turkistan. He dispatched a further forty under the leadership of *Maulana Furuh Hussein* to Arabia, The Yemen, Syria and Anatolia. He sent another ten persons from those who had reached the spiritual rank of perfection (*kamal*) to Kashgar, led by *Maulana Muhammad Sadiq*. A further thirty people he sent to the area of Turkistan, Badakhsan and Khurasan[10] under *Shaykh Ahmed Bakri*. They all achieved spectacular successes in the localities they were sent to, with great masses of people benefiting from their knowledge and guidance.

The assembly of people around the Imam was growing day by day. In fact, due to the great gathering and thronging of people around the Imam, the notables of the political establishment were even facing difficulties in being able to visit him. It wasn't long before the sultan became apprehensive of the deep attachment of the people to the Imam, causing him to summon the Imam in the year 1619 C.E. to the capital city of Agra. The sultan began to question him regarding certain sufi explanations appearing in one of the Imam's letters but was convinced with the rational explanations the Imam provided for them.

The matter may well have ended there, if not for certain close advisors to the sultan inciting against the Imam saying – "This Shaykh didn't bow to you in greeting and he has many followers within the army. He may soon arouse sedition amongst his followers and harm your kingdom. As long as Shaykh Ahmed has many followers within the army, he may march out against you and claim sovereignty for himself."

Most of the viziers of the sultan and government officials at that time had embraced ungrounded beliefs. This being the case, they were extremely vexed from Imam Rabbani's *Maktubaat*[11] in which he showed the shortcomings and criticism of deviant and corrupt beliefs. They were amongst those inciting the sultan against him.

As a result of this intrigue, sultan Jehangir ordered the arrest of Imam Rabbani (r), who had now reached 55 years of age, in the *Kufaayaar* Fort. His books, garden, well and house were confiscated, and his family had to relocate to another location.

The Imam took to educating the prisoners on Islam and guiding them to righteousness for the year that he was imprisoned and was a cause for some of them even entering Islam. While he himself, due to the sufferings and pains he was patiently bearing in the way of Allah (swt), advanced spiritually.

After the passing of a year in incarceration, the sultan regretted how the Imam was being dealt with and ordered the release of the Imam on the condition that he remained under house arrest in an army camp. The sultan also requested from Imam Rabbani (r) that he become his advisor in issues of religion, which the Imam took on for some time. The sultan became acquainted with the Imam's righteousness and sincerity through his request of the following stipulations from the sultan:

1. That the sultan abolishes the prostration of greeting and submission towards him.
2. That every masjid that was destroyed or damaged be rebuilt and repaired.
3. To abolish the edicts which prohibited the slaughter of cows.
4. That he supervises the judges, *muftis*[12] and officials of the state so that they all apply the rulings of Islam in their roles.
5. That he re-establishes the *jizya*[13] tax.
6. That he further annuls every *bida'*[14] and applies the Islamic Shariah.
7. That he orders the release of all those imprisoned only because of their religion.

It was clear from these requests that *Imam Rabbani* (r) did not ask for any personal interest. Rather his one goal was averting the sabotage and corruption perpetrated against Islam under the previous sultan and mitigating against a possible repeat of such corruption by a future sultan.

The Imam deemed it a great and precious opportunity that he had the ear of the sultan to encourage him upon the foundations of the Islamic faith. He began attending the sultan's gatherings and would speak of Islamic issues and those present would pay great attention to his words.

The sultan who was initially criticised because of his silence in the early period of his rule when some *masajid* were destroyed, now began building *masajid* due to the blessings of these gatherings and attached himself closer with Islam.

The Imam remained at the side of the Sultan for a period of 4 years. He remained writing letters to his disciples and friends during this time. In the year 1033 *hijri*, when he was returned his complete freedom, the Imam returned with his children, who had arrived to visit him, back to Sirhind. He spent the last year of his life, here in his hometown.

FOLLOWING OF THE SHARIAH BEFORE ALL ELSE

Imam Rabbani (r), who was watching with great agitation the deep infiltration of innovations (*bida'*) and deviations into the life of the Muslims, exerted untiring effort to return to the applying of the laws of Allah (swt). He had dealt with this matter considerably in his gatherings, letters and books. The Imam (r) says:

'*The Shariah has 3 parts; knowledge, action and sincerity. It is not possible to apply the Shariah except with realising these three. And once the Shariah is applied, then Allah's* (swt) *approval will be acquired, which surpasses the happiness of this world and the Hereafter together! As Allah* (swt) *says, "...**But Contentment from Allah is greater**..."*.[15] *The Shariah secures* *both the happiness of this world and the Hereafter together and we are not in need of any other objective.*

As for tariqa[16] and grasping realities (haqiqah), to which the Sufis dedicate themselves to, it is nothing but service to the Shariah. Wherewith it perfects and completes the third aspect of Shariah, that is, sincerity. Therefore, the intention behind tariqa and haqiqah is completion of the Shariah and hence there is nothing without the Shariah.

Indeed, the spiritual states, intuitions of the heart (ilhaam), spiritual sciences and knowledge gifted to the Sufis throughout their spiritual journeying and life-paths is not the objective nor the purpose on its own. On the contrary, these are all imaginings and delusions of the people of tariqa who have submitted themselves to the path of sufi disciplining. It is necessary to pass through all these states and affairs (not to get caught up with them) and to arrive beyond them to the station of acquiring the Good-Pleasure of Allah (swt). This is the end of the stations of the spiritual journey of the sufi path. The goal of traversing the stations of tariqa and haqiqah is not for anything other than acquiring ikhlas (sincerity) which is regarded as absolutely necessary to arrive at the station of Allah's (swt) Good-Pleasure.'

Knowledge is crucial. However, it should lead people to *taqwa* (righteousness or God-consciousness), that is carry them to the fear of Allah (swt) and guide them to the recognition of Him, as it is stated in the verse of the Quran, '**...only those among His servants who know, fear God...**'[17]

So, it is upon the servant that he acts according to his knowledge, and yet it is obligatory that he fulfils his actions with sincerity as deeds are not accepted except when accompanied by sincerity. *Dhu'l Noon al-Misri* [18](r) mentions:

'*All people are dead except those with knowledge, and all those with knowledge are sleeping except those that act (on their knowledge), and all those that act are deceived except those that are sincere! And the sincere are in grave danger!*'

In short, knowledge, action and sincerity are complementary elements to one another.

Imam Rabbani (r) would say that the *Shariah* and Sufism *(tassawuf)* do not contradict each other, and to clarify he would recollect the saying of Baha-ud-din Naqshbandi[19]:

"*What is intended from the Sufi path is the occurrence of complete ma'rifa (knowledge of Allah*(swt)*)*"

In accordance, *tariqa* is arrival to the understanding of the reality of the *Shariah* and it is not distinct from it nor from reality. Further, what is inner completes and perfects what is outer and hence it is not appropriate to accept statements from Sufis that are contradictory to the literal meaning of the *Shariah* nor to the consensus of the scholars of the people of Sunnah.

And Imam Rabbani (r) would say, "*Truly spiritual states are judged by the Shariah, as for the Shariah it is not judged by spiritual states. Since the Shariah is authentic and certain and its soundness is based on revelation. As for the spiritual states, they are presumptions and is only based on kashf (spiritual uncovering of knowledge) and knowledge of the spiritual states.*"

The Imam would also say in his letters:

"O my son. Spend your time in the remembrance of Allah(swt) *continuously. And every deed fulfilled according to the honourable Shariah is also included under remembrance even if it be buying and selling. Abidance to the laws of the Shariah are imperative at all moments of activity and repose so that they all become remembrance. Because remembrance is the absence of heedlessness and as long as you observe the commands and prohibitions in all your actions, then success from the chains of heedlessness is made easy and the continual remembrance of the Most High* (swt) *is obtained."*

Imam Rabbani (r) would also advise giving attention to *tassawuf* after learning the (external/literal) sciences of the *Shariah*:

"Truly the purpose of entering into tassawuf is the ability to fulfil righteous actions with ease and facility, do away with laziness, stubbornness and challenging similar reprehensible characteristics arising from the nafs al-amara (a person's evil-commanding ego or subconscious)."

"It is imperative to attend to the inner (development of a person's being) after adorning and beautifying the exterior with fulfillment of the laws of the Shariah. Otherwise actions will be muddled with heedlessness. Embellishing the exterior with the laws of the Shariah without aid from the interior is unfeasible."

"The role of the scholars is providing fatawah (legal edicts), while the work of the people of Allah(swt) *is righteous actions. And engagement with the interior self requires engagement with the exterior self. As for one who is concerned with the interior yet neglects the exterior, he is an irreligious heretic and the internal*

spiritual states he acquires are nothing but traps and lures for him[20]. The sign of the soundness of one's internal, spiritual state is adorning one's external self with the commands and prohibitions of the Shariah – and that is the straight path."

To sum up, the exterior and interior are two complementary elements one to the other and attention to only one, would keep the other deficient no matter one's advancement.

AHL-UL-SUNNAH WAL-JAMAA'H[21]

Corrupt ideas and false currents of thought had increased and aggravated to a great degree in the time of Imam Rabbani (r). The belief of many Muslims was shaken and challenged vehemently, and their worship and mutual dealings were corrupted. The Imam was clearly grieved and affected by the states of these Muslims and exerted great efforts in educating people and ensuring they be acquainted with the way of a*hl-ul-sunnah wal-jamaa'h* and return to it anew. He would write letters without fatigue or boredom and despite the grumblings and apathy in the face of his encouragement to hold fast to the beliefs of *ahl-ul-sunnah wal-jamaa'h* again. Rather, he would explain with detail and precision and would refer to the books of *fiqh (Islamic Jurisprudence or Law)* for details combined with his understanding of prevailing conditions.

The Imam advised that every spiritual guide (*murshid*) should direct new disciples associating with them, to not pay even the smallest value to opinions and spiritual unveilings which are contradictory to the Noble Quran and *hadith*, even if the difference appears trivial. In addition, the guide should verify the disciple's creedal beliefs (*aqeeda*) and that it is in accordance with the *aqeeda* of *ahl-ul-Sunnah* and teach them the necessary rules of *fiqh* (jurisprudence) and insist they act by them.

Imam Rabbani (r), for his part, would have his disciples read various books of *fiqh* originating from the scholars of religion and would insist and remind his representatives in far off lands via his letters '*Al-Maktubaat*', to make their own students and disciples read such books.

Some of these books included; in the field of Quranic Exegesis (*tafsir*): '*Tafsir Baydawi*'; in *hadith*: '*Sahih Bukhari*' and '*Miskhat al-Masaabih*', in *fiqh*; Al-Bazdawi and '*The Hidayah*', in *aqeeda*; '*Sharh al-Muwaaqif*' and '*Haashiyat-ul Adwadi*' and in *tassawuf*; '*Awarif al-ma'aarif*'.

Despite the Imam's (r) memorising of the topics of fiqh, deep understanding of them and his proficiency in *usul-al-fiqh*, he would hasten to clarify any *fiqhi* issue by referencing the dependable books of *fiqh* as a caution against falling into an error. He would never desist from these books and would act in accordance with the legal verdicts and opinions of the great scholars.

HIS ATTENTIVENESS AND KEEN OBSERVANCE IN FOLLOWING THE PROPHET'S(S) *SUNNAH*

Imam Rabbani (r) was a dedicated follower to the *Sunnah* of the noble Prophet(s) in every nuance, whether the issue was major or minor and would advise everyone to follow this course.

Once, a student of his requested permission to write the voluntary and daily prayers (*duas*), litanies *(wirds)* and prayers upon the Noble Prophet(s) (*salawat*) which he would perform. The Imam replied,

"The actions of priority that are followed are the actions of the Messenger (s) of Allah (swt). So, bring a book of hadith and learn from it!"

And when the student insisted on his request by saying, "Master! Your deeds are conforming to the actions of the Messenger (s) of Allah (swt)."

The Imam replied, "Write then but be very attentive. Write only that which is in conformity with the Sunnah – by deed and speech. Do not write anything contradictory to it!"

HIS WORSHIP

Just as the Imam himself was a great devotee to acts of worship (*ibadaat*) he would advise his students likewise for them to increase their concern for it. He would say: "*Despite the fact that the Prophet (s) was the beloved of Allah* (swt) *and he reached the highest degree and level (of closeness to Him* (swt)*), yet he would devote himself to worship of his Lord* (swt) *and lengthen his prayers until his feet would swell. Further, the 'people of truth' who follow, in the best manner, the truth of his way, act as he (s) acted. Hence, the more one increases in his obedience and worship of Allah* (swt)*, the more he becomes closer to Him* (swt)*.*"

The Imam saw the necessity of observing the voluntary actions *(nawafil)* together with the compulsory actions *(faraaid)* as they are great bounties that a Muslim should possess and be steadfast upon. The Imam, whether he was at home or upon a journey, in summer or winter, would awaken from his sleep after a half or two-thirds of the night had passed and read the *Sunnah duas* (prayers) especially for that time. Then he would make *wudu* (ablution) with much diligence, observing all its etiquettes. He would not request of anyone to pour the water of *wudu* for him, rather, would charge himself over it, would observe great concern that no water be wasted and would ensure with dedication that he was facing towards the direction of the *qibla* during *wudu*. However, when it came time to washing his feet, he would turn to face another direction (out of respect to the *qibla).* He would utilise the *miswak* (a natural toothbrush) at every wudu. He would wash the body-parts of *wudu* with great care, and every time he would wash a body part, would wipe it with his hands until there didn't remain the possibility of any trickling of water from the washed limb nor from his hands, and would do such as a precaution against the disagreement of the scholars around the validity of the purifying nature of water that has already been used once in wudu. Finally, during *wudu,* he would repeat the *duas* mentioned in the noble hadith of the Prophet (s).

After completing his *wudu*, he would recite the *dua* of *tahajjud* (the optional night prayer) and begin his prayer. Fulfilling it with presence of heart, complete submission and would recite within it the lengthy *surahs* (chapters of the

Quran). At the beginning of his night prayer, the Imam would recite *Surah Yaseen* repeatedly. While later into the night, he would tend to recite the Quran in order as much as possible. After the completion of his *tahajjud* prayers, the Imam would be lost in spiritual contemplations about Allah (swt) (*muraqabah*), reflection and meditation and complete submission and concentration would overcome him. He would then sleep for a short, designated period before the dawn prayer *(fajr salat)* as was the prophetic sunnah, then awake before the whitening of morning, refresh his *wudu* and complete the *(fajr)* prayer.

He would perform the *sunnah* prayers of *fajr* at home and would repeat silently in the interluding time between the *sunnah* and *fard* prayer the invocation; '*SubhanAllahi wa bihamdihi, subhanAllahil-Alzeem*' (Glorified and Praised be Allah! Allah the Magnificent be Glorified!). After the performance of the *fajr* prayer in congregation, he would complete his daily litanies (*awraad*) in the *masjid* with his companions until the time of *shurooq arrived (*once the sun has sufficiently risen*)*. Whence he would perform four cycles of the *ishraaq* prayer in sets of two and recite within them lengthy *surahs*. Afterwards, he would engage himself in transmitted and reliable *duas* and glorifications particular to that time.

It was then his habit to go to his house to see to the conditions of his wife and children and speak with them of the necessary daily duties before entering his room and busying himself with the recitation of the noble Quran. Afterwards, he would invite his students and question them about their affairs and deliver recommendations and advises that would motivate them to aim for the higher goals – i.e. the following of the prophetic *sunnah*, continuance of remembrance and contemplation of Allah (swt), concealment of their spiritual states from people and reading of the books of *fiqh*.

The Imam (r) would spend most of the time in gatherings and congregations in silence and would exert great care to not be involved in backbiting of others nor in finding the faults of fellow Muslims. Nor would those close to him slip into backbiting in his presence due to what they felt of honour and awe towards him. The Imam would also show great concern in concealing his (lofty) spiritual states from others (to guard one's self against showing off or being overtaken by love of fame etc...).

The imam would pray eight cycles of the voluntary forenoon prayer (*salat al-duha*) in his room before sitting with his wife and children for breakfast. If one of his children or workers were not present at this time, he would set aside their portion of food and keep it for them.

During times of eating he would be largely preoccupied with feeding others and questioning them of their conditions and affairs and would not sit at the table until and only if he felt a need for food and it was clear he was following a prophetic tradition (in eating less).

After lunch, he would withdraw for the short midday nap, also in obedience to the prophetic sunnah and after the postnoon prayer *(zuhur)*, would listen to the recitation of a part of the noble Quran from one of its memorisers. If there was a scheduled lesson, he would deliver it to his students.

He would perform the afternoon prayer *(asr)* at its earliest time and never leave its *sunnah* component[22]. After the conclusion of the prayer, he and his students would be preoccupied in silent spiritual contemplation and thought.

He would perform the sunset prayer *(maghrib)* also at its earliest time and after the fard prayer, before beginning his lesson, would recite ten times the formula, '*la ilaha ilalAllahu wahdahu la shareeka lah (There is no God but Allah alone and no partners does He have.)*'. After performing the sunnah of *maghrib* he would pray the prayer of the oft-repentant *(awaabeen)*[23].

As for the *witr salat*, the Imam would generally recite *Surah A'la*[24] in the first *rakat* (cycle), *Surah Al-Kafiroon*[25] in the second and *Surah Al-Ikhlas*[26] in the third. Sometimes he would perform the *witr* salat after the night prayer (isha) and sometimes after the night vigil prayer (*tahajjud*).

The Imam would observe all the *sunnahs* in his prayer as well as the recommended action, and etiquettes and show great concern in performing two *rakaats* after *wudu* and upon entering in the *masjid*.

He would retire for sleep directly after finishing the *isha* prayer, reciting the prophetic duas before sleep, increasing in *dhikr* (remembrance of Allah) and prayers upon the Prophet (s) - particularly increasing in the latter on the nights of Friday and Monday. He would advise and recommend insistently, those in his service and those who would consistently accompany him, with increasing in their concern for remembrance and contemplation (of Allah).

As for those listening to his recitation of the Noble Quran, then they would reach deep understandings of the secrets and wisdoms of the Quran. His manner and mode of recital, whether in or outside of prayer would be in accord with the verse's meaning, a style suited to the more frightening verses and another style for those inducing bewilderment or astonishment in men's hearts. As if the meaning of those verses were being manifested in his voice and noble countenance. He was persistent in the recital of the Noble Quran even on his journeys, while moving or resting.

He would show particular attention in the noble month of *Ramadan* and complete the recitation of the Quran at least three times in this month. He would hasten to break his fast and delay having the pre-fast meal *(suhoor)* in accordance to what has appeared in noble prophetic traditions. He would also seclude himself in a masjid *(ikhtikaf)* for the last ten days of the holy month.

As for the alms tax *(zakat)*, he would attend to it with great sympathy and attentiveness. Whenever a gift came to him, he would hurry to calculate its value without waiting for the lapse of a complete year[27] and pay its *zakat* hurriedly. He prioritised giving of the *zakat* to the workers in the fields, those busy with guiding and reforming the people, widows and divorced women, the needy and relatives. Likewise, he would visit the sick and elderly and recite beside them the transmitted *duas*, he would respond to invitations as long as they weren't gatherings in which sins and crimes would be committed.

The repetitions of Allah's (swt) praises and glorifications would not be separated from the tongue of Imam Rabbani (r) and he would thank Allah (swt) excessively even upon small blessings. He was abundant in *istighfaar* (seeking Allah's (swt) forgiveness) even when busy with performing good deeds. And when tested by a calamity or trial would say, 'This trouble is only because of my evil states and deeds'. He would look at that trial as a purification from sin like soap cleanses filth and would say that facing trials with contentment and acceptance is a reason for spiritual progress and elevated rank.

And although his life was full righteous deeds and abundant worship, he would have unparalleled humility and would look at himself as constantly being deficient.

HIS ADMIRABLE CONDUCT

Righteous and generous behaviour such as tenderness, humility, mercy and kindness to the creations of Allah (swt) and contentment with everything that befalls one from Allah (swt) had reached the highest degree in the heart of Imam Rabbani (r). The Imam and his family faced many grievances at the hands of the officials of government yet never begrudged against anyone nor complained – not even a word. As he was continually in a state of contentment, he would also advise his close companions on the same patience and contentment.

He would act in the most kind and mellow manner with others, if someone came to visit him, he would rise in honour for them, and make them sit at the front of his gathering and speak with them sweet words and in accordance to their spiritual state. He would be the first to give the greeting of *salaam* and was very concerned and mindful regarding the rights of people. When news came to him about someone's passing away, he would ask Allah's (swt) Mercy for them and recite the words of Allah(swt); **'Indeed to Allah we belong and to him we return'**.[28] He would participate in the funerals, praying and reciting Quran for the deceased.

On Fridays, for the *jumuah* prayer he would wear his most graceful robes as well on the two festivals *(eids)*. If he bought a new robe, he would first offer it to one of his disciples or family members. Most of the time, fifty to sixty people would have gathered around him, sometimes reaching a hundred. These gathering consisted of scholars, *arifeen*[29], spiritual guides, memorisers of the Quran as well holders of high political positions – and he would offer them all food from the kitchen of his house.

Imam Rabbani (r) held great respect for the Islamic rites and symbols. One day he saw one of the memorisers *(huffaz)* of the Noble Quran beginning his recital sitting on a mattress lower than his own mattress, so he immediately arose and sat at a place lower than the reciter. His high humility was also clearly apparent in the way he wrote his letters and books and he presented himself as *faqir* (a poverty-stricken or needy one – i.e.

needy of Allah in all things) or *dervish*. He wrote in one of his letters:

'This needy soul wants to put himself in the service and support of Islam and to struggle on this path to the most of his ability and potential and I hope, according to the hadith, 'Whoever imitates a people is of them', that this weak, incapable servant is allowed within this group. I am like the old woman who came with her yarn to the market in which our master, the Prophet Yusuf (a) was offered for sale so that she may purchase him with it.' (i.e. to purchase the most valuable of things (closeness with Allah) with the cheapest of things (his own soul)).

IMPOTENCE OF THE INTELLECT AND THE NECESSITY FOR PROPHETS

Imam Rabbani (r) held the human intellect and inspired-intuition *(ilhaam)* as incapable of understanding the Being and Attributes of Allah (swt) in their true realisation nor in a manner befitting of them nor in grasping realities in a complete sense. That it is not possible that most of the results and understandings achieved through the intellect or intuition be completely free from the risk of doubt, confusion, error, loss and negligence.

Hence, getting to the correct understanding of life and the universe and pure recognition of Allah (swt) is not possible except through the Prophets (a) since revelation flows upon them. Revelation is regarded as the fundamental source for absolute truth. Just as the power and strength of the human mind and the power of understanding and grasping ideas is distinct from the other senses like sight and hearing and above their capability, likewise the ability, capabilities and soundness of the Prophets (a) are above the capability of the mind. Hence none can direct us to the correct way of glorifying Allah (swt) nor to His worship nor to obedience of divine directives except the Prophets (a).

The philosophers who, with their embracing of the idea that the mind is an entity with infinite power and strength to arrive at realities, began measuring everything with its standard and fell into grievous and even ridiculous errors on the issue of knowledge of Allah (swt).

Just as there is not a pure and whole intellect, likewise there is no pure and whole spiritual intuition *(ilhaam)*, free from the desires and whims of the self *(nafs)* nor from external influences that direct to good or evil. Like a phoenix – it may exist in imagination but has no existence in the realm of reality.

As for the *ishraqis*[30], they claimed the truths of reality shine from within the soul of man and hence (more brightly) from those who attend to purifying and cleansing their souls *(nafs)* with just spiritual exercises and contemplations. They also fell victim to the snare of whims, doubts and ignorance.

To say that the intellect is wholesome and perfect and free from defects is inaccurate. That is because it is affected by one's convictions, faith-based thought and external factors. Nor is it possible to be free from weak points that affect one's thinking such as greed, covetousness, anger, animosity desires and the like. Nor is the intellect free from characteristics of deficiency such forgetfulness, misjudgement and absent-mindedness. Thus, we can say there are many judgements that human intellects have arrived to and they share openly with the world but are mixed and shaded with such blemishes. Hence the intellect is not a source of knowledge that is free from error. On the contrary, it is incompetent and is characterised by its lack of adequacy.[31]

On the other hand, the angel that brings down revelation to the Prophets and Messengers (a) is far from all these shortfalls and not affected by any of these negative factors. Consequently, prophethood is the only source that can be said to be free from deficiency, error or negligence and without it, true purification of the soul *(nafs)* is not possible.

The great Muslim historian and sociologist *ibn Khaldun* says on this topic: '*The intellect is a sound tool, its judgements certain and faultless – as long as you are not tempted to judge the details of (faith) like oneness of Allah(swt) (tawhid), the Hereafter, the realities of Prophethood, the realities of the Divine Attributes - as well as everything else beyond its limit – for that is desire of the unreachable. It is like a man who sees a scale balance which is weighing gold. So, after seeing its (limited scale of) precision, he desires to use it to weigh a mountain! This doesn't indicate that the scale is inaccurate in and of itself (but rather it is being misused). Likewise, the intellect has a limit in its ability to comprehend, discover and understand – it stops with this limit and doesn't overstep it.*"[32]

Philosophy and its corresponding ways claim to seek knowledge and understanding of realities without the need for the guidance of the Prophets (a). However, these realities cannot be known or understood except through means of the exceptional servants of Allah (swt), whom He has honoured with the advantage of prophethood. They are to be considered the greatest blessing Allah (swt) has bestowed on all humans. As the greatest sciences forwarded to humankind, i.e. those dealing with the essence of Allah (swt) and His Attributes – without waiting from man even the smallest compensation – are not possible for any people to arrive at, even a simple detail of them, through the methods of philosophical thought, research, study, experimentation, spiritual uncovering and neither through (methods of enlightenment based on) advancing and purifying the self *(nafs)* – even if they continued in that for thousands of years.

"*...That is from the bounty Allah has bestowed upon us and upon mankind, but most of mankind do not give thanks*".[33]

GOD'S ONENESS *(TAWHID)* AND CONTINUAL REMEMBRANCE *(DHIKR)*

Imam Rabbani (r) says regarding the high status of the declaration faith (*kalima al-tawhid*[34]):

'*I found the pure kalima (declaration of faith/shahada) to be a key to a treasure of ninety-nine mercies of Allah* (swt) *– that is, it is made into a rich repository for the Hereafter. I know that there is nothing more healing than these wholesome words in deflecting the darknesses of disbelief (kufr) or the turbidity of shirk (considering anything as a partner with Allah). No one in the coun-*

try has a desire like my desire – to sit in a zawiya (sufi lodging/ tekke) secluded from people, finding delight and happiness by repeating this blessed declaration – but we don't do as such. Not all dreams are made possible. There must be heedlessness and mixing with people...'[35]

Imam Rabbani (r) would continually advise people on the status of *dhikr* (remembrance of Allah (swt)):

'The seeker of this path, after correcting his beliefs (aqaaid) to be in accordance with the people of truth – thanks be to Allah (swt) for their efforts – and after learning the rules of fiqh as well as acting by what he learns, should devote all his time in the remembrance (dhikr) of Allah (swt). With the condition that the dhikr is taken from a complete and accomplished shaykh as perfection is not derived from what is deficient. It is incumbent that he is busy in dhikr whether with ritual ablution (wudu) and without wudu, standing or sitting and not leave it off whether he is coming or going or eating or sleeping.'

'Be conscious and take note that your well-being, rather the well-being of all the children of Adam (a) and their salvation and deliverance – is all connected with the remembrance of their Lord (swt). Therefore, one should be absorbed in the Divine remembrance as much as possible. Heedlessness cannot be – not even for a single moment!'

THE HALAL MORSEL

Imam Rabbani (r) says:

'My advice to you all is to have caution over food. A person shouldn't eat everything he finds, wherever he finds it, without first observing whether it is Islamically permissible or not. Human beings were not created purposelessly that they do whatever they wish, rather they have a God (swt) *who has entrusted them with commands and prohibitions and clarified what pleases Him and what doesn't through the vessel of prophets (a) who are a mercy to creation. The one deprived of happiness is he who walks a path contrary to his Lord's pleasure and acts in His dominion and kingdom without His permission and approval...'*

'The performance of the five prayers in congregation are necessary as well as preferring the permissible (halal) over the forbidden (haram)...one should also disregard fleeting pleasures and desires.'

THE IMPORTANCE OF GOOD COMPANIONSHIP

The Imam would continually recall the importance of companionship in the *Naqshbandi* way, being one of its crucial foundational principles. The following incident was narrated by *Khawaja Ahrar* (r):

'We were with a group of dervishes and began discussing the moment of Fridays in which prayers are answered. If it was attained what should be asked from Allah (swt) *in it? Every man put forth his ideas and I said – the company of the 'arbab al-jamiyya'* [36] *should be asked for. For all goodness is made easy within their midst...'*

Imam Rabbani (r) elucidates on the importance of right companionship in other letters of his book, *Al-Maktubaat*, saying:

'Do not equate right companionship with anything else, whatever it may be. Don't you see that the companions of the Messenger (s) excelled all others – except the prophets (a) – by virtue of their companionship? Even Owais al Qarni (r) and Umar ibn Abdul-Aziz Al-Marwani (r) didn't match their stations even though these two had reached the highest (spiritual) levels and arrived at such perfection...and if Owais al Qarni knew the advantage of companionship in this manner, nothing would have prevented him from companionship (of the Messenger(s)) and he wouldn't have preferred anything over its bounty...'

TAKING ADVANTAGE OF THE OPPORTUNITY (OF LIFE)

Imam Rabbani (r) would look at the life of this short world as a great opportunity and would advise his students to work towards taking advantage of it in the greatest way possible. He mentions in one of his letters:

'My dear son, the opportunity is to be seized! It is imperative that the whole of one's life not be spent in matters that are of no benefit. Rather, it is incumbent that the whole of one's life be spent in seeking the good pleasure of Al-Haqq (swt).[37] The five prayers should be performed in congregation according to its pillars, salat al-tahajjud (the optional late night prayer) should

never be abandoned, nor should the seeking of forgiveness in the early morning hours be so carelessly given up, neither should one be deceived by the fortunes of this worldly existence and death together with the horrors of the hereafter should be firmly kept in one's mind and remembrance.

In short, it is required that one be averse to this worldly life, devoted to the hereafter, is busy with this world only to the extent of necessity and spends the rest of his time working for the matters of the hereafter. The heart must also be devoid of being under the charm of any other than Allah (swt) and that one's outer being be beautified and adorned with the rules of the Shariah. This is the matter in essence – other than it is imaginations – and all other, resulting conditions will be good and in tranquillity.'

The Imam mentions in another letter:

'In accordance with the principle – what cannot be completely achieved should not be completely abandoned – it is necessary that dealings with others and seeking livelihood is persevered with throughout our short lifetimes in accordance with the Sunnah and following the bearer of the Shariah (s). For to be delivered from the punishment of the hereafter and winning eternal blessings is tied to the observance of this way...'

'Indeed, the time of action is the period of youth. The intelligent one is he who doesn't lose this time and seizes the opportunity. The matter is uncertain and perhaps one will not live to see old age and if he does then perhaps he will not be able to join good company and if he can then perhaps he will not be able to perform deeds since he is now of an age distinguished by weakness and impotency. However, the means for attaining good company

are all easy now (in youth)...Truly the best time for action and seizing opportunities is the time of strength and ability. With what excuse is the work of today delayed till the morrow and procrastination preferred?'

'My dear brother, now is the time for action! It is not time for words and empty talk. It is necessary that the heart is bonded with Allah (swt) *externally and internally. One must not consider other than Allah* (swt) *without His permission. This is true action and everything other than it is just chatter and smoke.'*

"My dear brother! Time is spent in working (for this world) yet every moment that passes, shortens something from one's lifespan and brings closer the designated time (of death). If vigilance is not acquired today, then the fortune of tomorrow will be with loss and regret. It is imperative that one establishes all their dealings according to the honourable Shariah in these limited days until he sees salvation. Truly this time is a time of action not a time of comfort. The relaxation which is the fruit of deeds is in front of us (in the hereafter) and relaxation in the time of work spoils farming and prevents the production of fruits.'

SELF-SACRIFICE AND RENUNCIATION

The abandonment of delights is the first condition for the advancement of the soul. It is not possible to arrive at Divine Love without desisting from the desires of the self. Imam Rabbani *(r)* expounded this reality saying:

'Truly the heart does not intertwine its love with more than one thing. So long as it is entangled with the love of any one thing,

it will not love another. Even if it is seen to have many desires and its love relates to many things around it such as wealth, children, leadership, praise, glory and status with people – in fact, its love is still only one and that is love for one's own self (nafs)! For what is the love of all these things except branches and manifestations of one's own love for one's own self. His desire for these things is founded in seeking interest for his own self, he doesn't seek those things in and of themselves. If this love for one's self passes, so too, consequently, passes the love for all other things.

Hence it was well said – Certainly the veil between the servant and the Lord is the self (nafs) of the servant – not the world itself. The world in its essence is not the goal of the human servant that it even be considered a veil. Indeed, the one desire of the servant is his own self. Most certainly, the veil between man and God is the servant's self, nothing else! As long as the servant doesn't renounce the desire of his self (nafs) completely, his Lord will not be his desire, nor will his heart accommodate the love of Allah (swt).'

Maulana Jalal al-din al-Rumi (r) says further:

'Intimacy with *Al-Haqq* (Allah) (swt) is not ascending to the highest of stations or being reduced to the lowest. Indeed, closeness to *Al-Haqq* (swt) is being free from the imprisonment of existence (i.e. of the self).'[38]

Imam Rabbani *(r)* delivered the following advice to his children so that this notion of freeing the heart from the love of transient creation and in its place direction towards divine love be ingrained in them:

'*It is vital that nothing other than what is pleasing to al-Haqq* (swt) *is pleasing and desirous for you. If we are to leave (this worldly existence), all these things leave from us. So, let them leave within our lives and don't consider them. Indeed, the friends of Allah* (swt) *(awliya) have left these matters by their own initiative (before death).'*

HIS DEATH

Imam Rabbani *(r)* started being subjected to difficulty in breathing a number of months before his death. In his last days he said to his children:

'Dear children, there is nothing left for me in this world that I direct my attention to or that binds me to it. Rather, contemplation of the eternal world overpowers me, and this alludes to the appointment for my departure which draws near.'

He then cut off all his relationships with the external world and preferred seclusion and solitude. He would not leave his isolation except to perform the five prayers in congregation and the Friday prayer. He would spend his entire time in remembrance of Allah (swt), seeking forgiveness and busying himself in (perfecting) his outer and inner self. This state of his was in accordance with what Allah (swt) mentions in His Venerated Book:

'So, remember the Name of thy Lord and devote thyself to Him with complete devotion.'[39]

Tears would accompany his eyes most times from the intensity of his longing to meet Allah (swt) and the phrase '*O Allah! (Please let me be with) the Highest Companion!*'[40] never left his lips. Several days passed in this manner and meanwhile his health and vigour somewhat returned, and peace and ease settled upon soft, uneasy and troubled hearts (of family and friends). As for the Imam, he began saying:

'I no longer feel, in these days of health, the pleasure and spiritual delight that I felt in my sickness!'

In these days he increased in charity and deeds of goodness and when one of his companions saw him giving much charity and performing many good deeds, he asked him, 'Is all this for the sake of repelling the calamity?'

The Imam would reply, *'No, not for the repelling of calamity. It is burning desire for reunion' (with Allah* (swt)*).*

Once his children saw him crying. On questioning him on the cause of his crying, he replied, *'I am crying out of happiness in meeting Allah* (swt)*!'*

When his children said to him, 'You have been acting unusually. You have stopped us from caring and attending to you in these final days. Why so?'

The Imam replied, *'The reason is the Love of Allah* (swt) *which is greater than your love!'*

As he neared to his time, he began depending on the infinite kindnesses of Allah(swt) and His blessings which cannot be enumerated nor adequately mentioned and began distributing all his robes to the poor and needy. Because he didn't have a thick, cotton robe to preserve him from the cold weather, his high temperature returned anew and the health of Imam Rabbani *(r)* broke down again. A similar incident happened with the Messenger (s) when he recovered from his sickness shortly before he passed and travelled to the Highest Companion (swt). It too happened with the Imam following this *Sunnah*.

The Imam did not give up the performance of the prayers in congregation till these last days when he encountered difficulties due to weakness and loss of his strength. He was continuously preoccupied with invocations, supplication and remembrance of Allah(swt) and was not heedless of His (swt) contemplation for even a moment. Nor was he negligent of the matters and principles of the *Shariah* nor of the sufi spiritual path and was consistent in the *tahajjud* prayer until his last night.

The Imam would advise those around him with following the *Sunnah*, being wary of falling into innovations and being continuous in remembrance and contemplation *(muraqabah)*:

'*Never did the possessor of this Shariah, our master, the Messenger (s) ever slacken, not even for a moment, on acting for the goodness of his nation (ummah) and striving for their rectification and their guidance in accordance with his principle – "Religion is naseehah. (advice, sincerity)"*[41] *– so it is necessary to follow the accepted religious texts and acting in accordance with them. Don't let a single sunnah pass you by!*"

And he said, requesting from his wife, 'It appears my travelling to the hereafter will be before yours. So, take the expenses of preparing the funeral from the wealth of your dowry.' As one of the most *halal* sources of wealth is the woman's dowry.

And the Imam would continuously be in a state of *wudu* because of his desire that death reach him in a state of *wudu*.

In his last moments, as he was restricted to his mattress, he would lay on his right side and put his right hand under his right cheek, following the prophetic *sunnah* and busy himself with remembrance of Allah (swt). When his children observed the hastening pace of his breathing they asked how he was feeling with the Imam only replying with - 'I am fine'. Thereafter he wouldn't repeat anything beside the majestic phrase – '*Allah*'. It was only a short moment after this, that his soul was delivered to its Creator (swt).

Our Imam (r) farewelled this transient world on the 18th day of the Islamic month of *Safar* in the year 1034 hijri corresponding to the 10th of December 1624 C.E. He was 63 years of age.

When the blessed body of Imam Rabbani *(r)* was brought for the burial washing, people found his hands folded over his chest as they are in the position of *salat*. The one washing his body separated his hands apart only to find they had returned to their initial position after the washing. Even after his shrouding, people saw again his hands still tied together in accordance with the prophetic *sunnah*. His children said, 'As long as the Imam wants it that way, we will let it be so!'.

As people cried around the body, there was a smile on the illuminated face of the Imam – words were incapable of describing its beauty. As if he was being portrayed by the poet when he said:

> *Your mother gave birth to you, son of Adam, crying*
> *And the people around you were laughing happily*
> *Take heed over your deeds so you are – when they cry*

On the day of your death – laughing joyfully.

The washing and shrouding were completed fully according to the prophetic sunnah. He was buried in his hometown, in the town of Sirhind, in the land of al-Hind (present-day India).

Truly, Imam Rabbani *(r)* was not a scholar restricted to his time. Rather he is amongst those scholars who are considered to be from the people of Allah (swt) and from those whose fame and light reached the entire world in his time and the times after him. He guided a great number of people to the true path and has continued to do so till this day through his works and books.

SOME OF HIS WISE ADVICES

"My son! The crux of the matter is avoiding excessive desire for those matters that are permissible and having contentment with only what is necessary of them. This necessary amount should be what is enough to acquire strength and stamina and the awakening and liveliness of the heart to be able to truly fulfil servitude to Allah (swt)*."*

* * *

"Time shouldn't be spent in pastime and games or wasting one's life aimlessly – not to mention spending it in forbidden matters. Beware of music and song and being deceived by enjoyment in it for it is a poison coated in honey.

You must abstain from backbiting and slandering among people as severe threats have been against these two reprehensible deeds. Also, abstaining from lying and defamation, for these two depravities are forbidden in all religions (i.e. their evils being so obvious). As for covering the faults and sins of others, forgiveness and overlooking their mistakes then these are from the (recommended) matters requiring great will and resolution."

* * *

"Truly, following the way of the prophets elevates one to the highest, spiritual level and following the chosen ones (of Allah's (swt) slaves) takes one to great spiritual stations. For Abu Bakr (r) strove for the complete approval of the Prophet (s), was continual in following the Prophet's way and hence was situated at the peak of the level of the siddiqeen (the truthful). As for the accursed Abu Jahl, he squandered his potential to follow (the Prophet) in the swamp of desires and passions of the nafs (self) and so became a forerunner of the cursed and damned."

* * *

"Surely, the scholars' love and desire for this lowly world is a defect and stain on the beauty of their status. If benefit is to result from their knowledge for people, it is not completely beneficial at the level that it should be. Therefore, what transpires from their supporting of the Shariah or strengthening the religion should not be given esteem. Support and strength may sometimes even be achieved from the people of immorality or callousness...However if the scholars are averse to this lowly world, liberating themselves from the shackles of love of wealth, leadership and love of fame and glory – then they are true scholars of the hereafter[42] and inheritors of the prophets (a) and amongst the best of creation."

* * *

"This world is a farmland for the hereafter. So, pity be upon he who doesn't sow it, who ruins the soil of predisposition (the goodness that is innate in every person) and loses the harvest of good action. It is known that the wastage of good land and its inactivity is because it hasn't been sowed or the seed planted is bad and rotten, the latter being more harmful and corrupt[43] – a fact not hidden from anyone."

* * *

"Know that the recitation of a surah from the Quran or a verse, revealed regarding a particular issue, brings about a benefit to its reader in that affair. For example, reading a verse connected with purification of the self leaves a great impression on people on the matter of cleansing and purification from the evil and repugnant characteristics of the self. It is likewise in relation to other issues." [44]

* * *

"Certainly, the reason behind the virtues and feats alleged to this poor soul, is precedence in supporting this religion and seniority in spending wealth and exertion of souls for the aid of the laws of the religion of the Lord (swt) *of all that exists. As the prophet* (s) *was the forerunner and preceded all in the aforementioned, so he was the most superior amongst all. Likewise, everyone who supersedes in this matter, is more virtuous than those behind him.*

* * *

"Without doubt, Allah (swt) *teaches his servants the following prayer:*
'(and who say) Our Lord! Grant us comfort in our spouses and our progeny and make us leaders (imams) for the reverent (muttaqeen)[45].

That is, it is not sufficient for man that he just possesses piety (taqwa) rather it is necessary that he exerts his effort to be a leader in piety (taqwa).

* * *

"Truly, the purpose of the human creation is only carrying out the service of slave-hood (uboodiyah) to Allah (swt). And he who is given infatuation (ishq) and love (for Allah (swt)) at the middle or beginning (of his spiritual path) then the objective of it is cutting off one's attachment to everything besides being at the side of His Sanctity, Allah (swt). So, infatuation (ishq) and love are not objectives in and of themselves, rather, they are a means to reach to the level of slave-hood.

Indeed, the spiritual traveller (salik) can only be a true slave to Allah (swt) if he eliminates being captive in servitude to anything other than Him (swt). Hence, there is no benefit in infatuation (ishq) other than it being a means to cut off everything other than Allah(swt). Therefore, the end of the levels of 'friendship with Allah' (wilayah) is the station of slave-hood. There is not a station of closeness with Allah above the station of slave-hood."

* * *

Footnotes

1. *Urfaan* –refers to a knowledge where one has a deeper knowledge of Allah (swt) and connection with Him.
2. In Sufi terminology, a shaykh's *khalifah* is his spiritual successor, substitute or representative.
3. Also known as *Rabee-ul-Thani* and is the fourth month of the Islamic calendar.
4. The Islamic pilgrimage to Mecca
5. The Muslims of the Prophet's Sunnah and Community
6. Creed/set of beliefs
7. *Imam Rabbani (r)* says about the likes of such scholars: "It is necessary that the people of Islam realise that the aid and support of the Muslim ruler is from amongst their obligations. This requires guiding the ruler towards honouring the *Shariah* and strengthening the Religion. Such support to the sultan can be various methods other than by word and deed. True, the most urgent and first matter is that of advice by speech. And the best of such speech is elucidating a matter of the *Shariah* or a tenet of *Aqedah* with what is consistent with the Quran and *Sunnah* and

consensus of the Muslim, Sunni scholars. By doing so, it prevents the ability of deceivers and innovators – who appear in society from time to time – from obstructing right guidance and corrupting the conditions of the people. This type of aid and support is specific for scholars of *ahl-ul-sunnah* who have put the Hereafter in their sights. That is because the companionship of scholars, whose entire concern is materialistic and consists of the procurement of all fleeting, worldly benefits, is a deadly poison. Their corruption goes beyond just themselves and spreads to others that are surrounding them. In actuality, the calamities that befell the earlier peoples occurred because of such corrupters. These are the ones who produced the misguided sultans and kings of foregone times. Nor were they satisfied with just the misguidance of rulers; indeed, these corrupt, deviant scholars became leaders to the misguided sects which have reached seventy-two in number. There isn't anyone whose deviance and misguidance affects others as much as corrupted scholars do. In fact, the bulk of ignorant ones who imitate and call themselves Sufis today are like such corrupt scholars. This is because their distorted and invalid ideas affect others not just themselves." *(Al-Maktubaat, 1, 243, Number 47 - Al-Imam Ahmed Al-Sirhindi.)*

8. Islamic legal verdicts. Singular: *fatwa*.
9. Sufi lodge.

10. Previously consisting of parts of Persia, Afghanistan and Central Asia.
11. The most renowned work of Imam Rabbani is his 3-volume collection of letters called *al-Maktubaat (Letters)*, written in mostly Persian and some Arabic consisting of letters to his students.
12. Islamic Scholars who deliver religious edicts. Singular: *mufti*
13. In Islamic Law; A minimal tax on non-Muslims living in an Islamic state if they can afford it. In return the state protects their lives and property from external and internal threats.
14. *Bida'*; an innovation in the rites, rituals or creed of the Islamic faith not sanctioned by the Prophet?
15. Quran 9:72. Translation from The Study Quran, Seyyed Hossein Nasr et al. 2015.
16. Referring to the sufi paths
17. Quran 35:28. Translation from The Study Quran, Seyyed Hossein Nasr et al. 2015.
18. A prominent Sufi saint from Egypt, 9th century, C.E.
19. Sufi saint and founder of the Naqshbandi Tariqa. From the town of Bukhara, Uzbekistan, 14th Century C.E.
20. Author's note: Such entrapping by Allah (swt) is the bestowing of blessings by Allah (swt) on misguided ones and granting them their spiritual wonders – only to increase them in their misguidance. Such traps can be similar to the miracles (*kiramaat*) of the *Awliya*

(Allah's (swt) chosen friends) but occur through the hands of disbelievers, the wicked and those who pretend to be shaykhs, even despite their corruption and misguidance. This type of state drives one to delusions. This is different to the real bringing closer of a person to Allah(swt), for He will distance him further away from such trials.

21. The people of the Sunnah of the Noble Prophet (s) and its community.
22. 4 cycles of recommended prayer before the 4 obligatory ones.
23. The prayer of the oft repentant. It consists of six cycles of voluntary prayer prayed after *maghrib salat*. Some scholars hold the opinion it is to be prayed in the forenoon between *fajr* and *zuhur*.
24. Chapter 87 of the *Quran*.
25. Chapter 109 of the *Quran*.
26. Chapter 112 of the Quran.
27. Generally, the *zakat* or tax on one's wealth meant for the poor is applicable on one's wealth that remains after the lapse of a complete year.
28. Quran; 2;156.
29. *Arifeen;* The spiritually adept that have a deeper knowledge of Allah (swt)
30. Appears to be a reference to the *ishraqi* school that mixed Sufism with philosophical thought.
31. Although the human mind is generally incapable of deducing many absolute truths, it is a great tool (when

not affected by the above-mentioned negative influences) to make balanced judgements to see which arguments are rational and/or probable and which are ridiculous. For example, the existence of a God-like being is among the most manifest and probable signs we see in the universe because of the all the interdependent complexities we see around us. For example, take the uniqueness of the human face. If we suppose it is 'nature' that creates it, nature should have knowledge of all faces living in the world today so as to give a new baby an unique and different face from all others. However, this knowledge must also extend to all past time and all future time – since each face is unique throughout time – making 'nature' all-knowing and all-knowledgeable. This is an example of how naturalists and evolutions take Allah's Attributes and assign them to other things. In the end, the existence of the Names and Attributes of Allah (swt) are undeniable and must be submitted too. After the existence of Allah is affirmed, this rationally leads to the existence of Prophets and Angels. (Derived from *'The Risale I Nur Collection'*, by *Bediüzzaman Saeed Nursi* (r) .

32. The Muqqadima, pg. 463. *ibn Khaldun*. (Arabic reference)
33. Quran; 12:38
34. That is, to say: There is no god but Allah, and Mohammed is His messenger.

35. That is, the Imam chose to carry the load of his responsibilities rather than seeking personal pleasures, even if that pleasure was linked a pious act like repeatedly remembering Allah (swt) in seclusion. Something one could have easily persuaded oneself to do.
36. A gathering in which the fervour of the sufi seekers are concentrated together for the purpose of seeking closeness to Allah (swt) and abandoning everything beside Him. In other words, it is the state of a gathering in which hearts have presence and spiritual attachment with Allah(swt).
37. 'The Truth'. Amongst the Names of Allah (swt).
38. Couplet 4514, Volume 3, Mathnawi, Maulana Rumi.
39. Quran; 73:8
40. Narrated to be the last words of Prophet Muhammad ?. See Bukhari 4437.
41. 95, Book of Imaan, Sahih Muslim.
42. What the Imam seems to be alluding to here is that Islam brings knowledge of the hereafter and what is beyond this material world. Therefore, its scholars belong to the hereafter in the sense that they are accustomed and knowledgeable with the realities of the hereafter and what is beyond this life and beyond death – in knowledge and action. If a scholar's goals are worldly then he falls short of this noble rank as he belittles this heavenly knowledge to the level of other worldly sciences.

43. A clear reference to hypocritical actions – those that have incorrect or insincere intentions. Or actions that may have good intentions but not performed with the Sunnah of the Prophet ﷺ in mind.
44. The Imam in his amazingly concise manner and great wisdom gives here a solution for Muslims overtaken by bad character traits and tested with calamities and trials. Not only does this method connect one with the *Quran* in their day to day life but also is a potent method for the reformation of the self and with dealing with the burdens of life. Verses that are read, ideally with understanding, and pertaining to a particular matter, open up the doors of divine assistance and offer succour and support to poor and impotent man. In the way of example, on dealing with lusts one may refer to and recite *Surah an-Naziat*, verses 34-46, on procrastination one may recite *Surah al-Asr*, on making all 5 prayers on time refer to *Surah al-Mudatthir*, verses 42-43 etc... One should refer to tafseer, translations, and asking of scholars for elucidation and greater understanding and hence receive greater effulgence and effect from these honourable verses. When the problem is more severe let him resort to greater doses of medicine and recite these verses with greater constancy and alongside *dua*, repentance and good deeds. And *Allah (swt)* knows best.
45. Quran [25:74]

CHAPTER 2

Wisdoms from Imam Rabbani - Part 1

Abdullah ibn al-Daylami (r) articulates the importance of being attached to the prophetic sunnah with perfect submission and obedience with his saying: "I have come to understand that the first of the religion to be neglected is the sunnah. The religion will be taken away sunnah by sunnah like a rope is taken away, pull by pull."

Imam Rabbani *(r)* says:
"Whatever of our sound worship is exerted for the good pleasure of Allah (swt), *our ability to do so is only from the favour of Allah* (swt). *If I must explain the reason for this, then I say that the cause of all grace is the connection with the Messenger (s) of Allah, who is the leader of the earlier and later generations, and acting in accordance with his tradition and blessed path...and the reason for the human not achieving a portion of something or*

not achieving it completely is only carelessness in a matter in the absolute following of the Messenger (s).

Once, I was overtaken by heedlessness and I entered the bathroom with my right foot (contradicting the way of the sunnah which is to enter with the left foot). I was held back that day from many advanced spiritual states".

It is not possible to attain the spiritual states which bring a slave closer to his Lord, except through complete submission and obedience to the Messenger *(s).* Our Lord(swt) proclaims in the honourable book:

"**Whosoever obeys the Messenger obeys God...**"[1]

"**Say (O Messenger) – If you love God, follow me, and God will love you and forgive you your sins...**"[2]

Hence, you are unable to arrive at the love of Allah (swt), except through the means of obedience to His beloved *(s)* and conceding to his way. Truly the door of divine Love is locked except for the one who would walk this path with the least hesitancy, doubts or negligence. The love of the Prophet *(s)* is love for Allah (swt), and obedience to him *(s)* is obedience to Allah (swt) and to disobedience to him *(s)* is akin to disobedience to Allah (swt) and this reality is founded upon Quranic verses. So the believer is compelled and obliged to correctly have his movement and his rest, his small actions and his great actions, to be all in accordance with the way and method of the beloved *(s)* of Allah who is considered to be the explainer of the noble Quran by his noble actions. So, let the believer have attentiveness and great care in following and observing the prophetic *sunnah*.

It is evident that, generally, the believers who hold on to the prophetic sunnah as their aim, have no negligence or drop in performing the compulsory actions *(faraa'id)*. On the opposite end, those that are negligent of the sunnah actions, may miss or be negligent of many compulsory actions also. Consciousness and attentiveness to the *sunnah* is regarded as a strong shield enveloping the compulsory actions which are the foundational pillars of religious life and protectors of it. That is why when satan the accursed and his helpers overwhelm the religion of man and his faith, they first act on distancing him from the prophetic *sunnah*. For they know if they are unsuccessful in this, then they have no hope or ambition in the compulsory actions either.

And so, *Abdullah ibn al-Daylami (r)* explained the importance of sticking by the prophetic sunnah completely with submission and obedience with his words:

'*It has come to my realisation that the first of the religion to be neglected is the sunnah. The religion will be taken away sunnah by sunnah like a rope is taken away, pull by pull.*'

Turning back from the *sunnah* and removing it from our lives would be like trying to make eternal happiness – God forbid – with a spindle for wool.

On referring to the history of religions, we find that the deviations and corruptions like those of the Jews and Christians began in this manner. They first abandoned and broke away from the example of the prophets. Thereafter, their beliefs and worship were corrupted. In the end, prayer was abandoned and in its place ritual and hymns were established. Fasting was abandoned and, in its place, limited diets were allowed[3]. Likewise, the veil (hijab) was abandoned and limited to only nuns – and even nuns have begun to abandon the veil and covering in our times.

It is necessary upon all of us that we, like true believers (*munimoon*), have alertness and piercing foresight in this matter. The enemies of religion today exert themselves in private and public and with all their strength to corrupt Islam, just like Christians were corrupted a foretime. They, in order that their true, hidden intentions do not come to light and become bare in front of people, do not direct their efforts in their initial schemes, towards corrupting the foundations and pillars of belief (*aqidah*) nor the compulsory actions. Initially, their focus is on lessening the importance of the *sunnah*, which is considered as a protective shield for those foundational principles and laws.

What is more grievous and serious, is that we stumble across many of these corrupting movements in our time that have spread ideas contradictory to the way of *ahl ul-sunnah wal-jama'ah*[4], which have shaken and corrupted the beliefs of many Muslims and spread deviation into their rites of worship and interactions. We find personalities who describe themselves as scholars of the religion and take on the appearance of teachers of theology and the *shariah*. However, they strive their utmost to poison hearts and destabilise ideas even in matters in which the *ummah* has agreed and gathered upon for 14 centuries!

These corrupters cite the rejection of miracles due to the inability of their deficient minds in understanding them and arriving to their essences[5]. They strive to critique and alter the (Islamic) legal tradition in accordance with their desires even resorting to *ijtihad* [6] and opinion in matters in which there is clear and absolute textual evidence. They reject the hadith which don't agree with their views – truly distant from the laws of *riwaya* and *sanad* [7] and neither do they grant the sunnah the importance earlier mentioned.

They forsake the prophetic *sunnah* which is an elaboration, exegesis, explanation and practical application of the noble Quran by raising the slogan of 'sufficiency of the Quran'. Which, appears outwardly, and at first glance, true and sound. They then attempt to bring about a 'Quranic Islam' particular to them and in tune with their desires, by their explanation of the Quran based on their ideas and opinions.

In fact, the Messenger *(s)* has already singled out this group as from amongst the deviators of the religion, who wear the garb of Islam and quote the Quran and appear to be upholders of it yet hide their true intentions and goals. This appears in the noble hadith:

"Beware! I have been given the Qur'an and something similar to it together! Yet the time is coming when a man, fed to his fill, sitting on his couch, will say – 'Keep to the Qur'an; what you find in it to be permissible treat as permissible, and what you find in it to be prohibited treat as prohibited.' – Beware! What the Messenger of Allah has forbidden is like what Allah has forbidden" [8]

In another transmission the Prophet *(s)* expounds the necessity of following the *sunnah*, he says:

*"Does any of you, while reclining on his couch, imagine that Allah has prohibited only that which is to be found in this Qur'an? By Allah, I have preached, commanded and prohibited various matters as numerous as that which is found in the Qur'an, or more numerous..."*⁹

The following verse from the Quran draws attention to the fact that it is not possible to understand the noble Quran in its true sense except through the way of prophetic sunnah. Allah, the Most High (swt), proclaims:

"Brought down by the trustworthy spirit. Upon thine heart (O Muhammad) – that thou may be among the warners – in a clear Arabic tongue."¹⁰

That is why penetrating to the secrets and hidden wisdoms of the noble Quran and understanding them is not possible except through scooping water from the spring of the heart of the Messenger (s) of Allah (swt). As the life of the Messenger (s), throughout the period of prophethood which extended to 23 years, was as a living explanation of the noble Quran.

From this respect, knowledge and understanding of the Messenger is the most important step on the path of slave-hood to Allah (swt). Without knowing the Messenger (s) and understanding him and travelling in his footsteps and path and learning from his compassion and sensitivities of heart, our faith is not complete. Neither is our slave-hood, and neither is understanding the noble Quran in its true sense.

There are many divine commands, about which their details on how to implement them in daily life, are not mentioned in the noble Quran. We cannot know such details except from how the Messenger (s) applied them in his life.

For example, there is the matter of eating *maytah* (an animal that is found dead). The noble Quran has generally forbidden the eating of *maytah* flesh. However, excluded from this prohibition are fish after they have been hunted. This exemption in known from the knowledge of the prophetic *sunnah*.

Likewise, the noble Quran mentions the commandment of prayer, except that it doesn't explain how it is to be performed. That is to say it doesn't clarify its details such as the number of cycles *(rak'aat),* the required Quranic chapters (*surah*) and prayers to be recited, arrangement of the prescribed parts of the prayer etc. and we are not aware of these matters except through the *sunnah*.

Other than that, the noble Quran uncovers its secrets and wisdoms to the people of *taqwa* (piety/God-consciousness). Allah (swt) says in the Quranic verse –

"This is the Book in which there is no doubt, a guide for those mindful of Allah (muttaqeen)."[11]

– referring to those who are cautious and wary of falling into forbidden things out of fear and awe to Allah (swt).

Hence, the best of those who understand the noble Quran and grasp its meanings are those who live their lives in *taqwa* and purify and mend their hearts. Any man or woman can sit in front of a copy of the noble Quran and read it, however, anyone only benefits from it according to the susceptibility of their heart.

Let us recount this high status of faith which the Commander of the Believers, *Umer ibn al-Khattab* (r) exhibited, and in which there are many lessons:

Umer (r) left his home one night to watch over the city of Medina. He passed by the home of a Muslim just as he was standing for prayer. Umer (r) stopped to listen to his recitation. He was reciting Surah al-Tur until he reached the verses:

"Truly, thy Lord's Punishment shall come to pass. None can avert it."[12]

Umer (r) said, '*By the Lord of the Ka'ba, a certain oath!*' He descended from his donkey and leaned on a wall, remaining there for a prolonged time. Then he left for his house but stayed a month on his bed out of the intense shock from the divine threat flowing from those verses. People would visit him yet be bewildered about his illness.[13]

The noble Quran is a vast ocean without bottom or shore. It's possible for one to be completely submerged in its depths depending on the level of one's heart. Just like someone who cannot swim cannot wade into deep waters while the skilful swimmer can plunge into a stormy ocean and reach its depths, where he witnesses a different world filled with strange and amazing spectacles that affect the heart and are not possible to witness from the coastline. The matter is similar for those who have traversed the advanced stations of the heart, following the way of *taqwa*. It is possible for them to witness many manifestations of the wisdoms and decrees of the noble Quran and attain the spiritual radiance of them through their true meanings and implications.

However, some miserable figures, without witnessing these realities and truths, dare to re-mould the religion – in the name of 'following the Quran' – in accordance with their shallow ideas and narrow opinions. They, who have not advanced to even the beginner levels of students of knowledge and *urfaan* (deep realisation), occupy themselves with directing criticisms to the great leaders of the *mujtahideen*[14] without the least amount of respect.

They adopt the opinion that 'Those men were scholars from a thousand years ago in the past. As for today, the times have changes aplenty'. Then they play with solid, religious injunctions which don't change with the change of the times. This approach is considered amongst the most dangerous from the actions of orientalists and missionaries to dismantle and destroy the religion. They are from the scum of the heedless who believe that religious knowledge is used in criticising and dismantling religion in place of supporting it.

Accordingly, it is imperative upon our youth, in particular those who pursue religious knowledge, that they be alert and cautious about whom they receive and learn their religious knowledge from. In fact, the Prophet (s) warned and advised his companion, *Abdullah bin Umar (r)*, as well as others he loved dearly:

*"O ibn Umar, your religion is **your religion**. It is your flesh and blood. So, pay attention from whom you take (it). Take it from those who are consistent and steadfast, not from those who diverge (from the right path or follow their desires).*

In actuality, the noble companions and the righteous believers (*muminoon*) who walked in their footsteps as well as those who were extremely cautious in this matter, would travel for knowledge continuously, bearing the burdens of travel in those times, in search of a single narrator of *hadith,* to confirm the narrator's uprightness and then take the *hadith* from him. They reached high levels of virtue due to prophetic guidance to the extent that one of them rejected a narrator and didn't take a *hadith* from him even after travelling a long distance because he saw the narrator pretending to offer food to his animal which had escaped in order to draw it near and catch it. The seeker of hadith deemed this action as a violation of proper conduct and didn't see someone who had an inclination for trickery – even if it be against an animal – as worthy of being a narrator of *hadith*. As he had not abided by, through his character and manner, to what was necessitated by the noble, prophetic *hadiths.*

Abu A'liya (r), who is considered one of the great imams of the *tabieen*[15] would say: 'We would come to a man to take *hadith* from him. We would look to see him pray and if he perfects it, we would sit near him and say (to ourselves) he is better than others. But, if he spoiled his prayer, we would stand up and say he is worse than others."

Today also, it is stipulated upon the leaders in knowledge to take their religious expertise in consideration of these standards. For truly, Allah (swt) the Truth says in His noble book: "**...Those truly fear Allah, among His Servants, who have knowledge...**"[16]

That is, the first condition that a true, knowledgeable scholar (alim) attends to is taqwa and fear of Allah (swt). For it is with this characteristic (fear of Allah), that Allah (swt) describes the scholars from amongst his slaves – not the heedless ones that suppose (Islamic) scholarship is without fear of Allah (swt) and without humbleness towards His Messenger (s). The heedless ones' only yardstick of measurement for the truth is their lacking minds with which they come forward and sift the religion, taking what is in harmony with their minds and desires and throwing away what is not!

Fundamentally, faith is a foundational acknowledgement requiring belief, from the heart, in many matters that leave the mind incapable of completely understanding and comprehending them. Just like the eye has a range of vision it cannot see beyond; the mind has limited capacity to understand and thus cannot comprehend everything.

This begs the question – Shouldn't there exists a reality to all matters of faith even if they are beyond the limits of the mind's capacity to understand them?

No doubt, the realities of religion will eventually reveal uncountable wisdoms and secrets to man, who has a limited mind and owns only partial knowledge due to the Originator of them being *Al-Haqq* (The Reality i.e. Allah) (swt), the Possessor of knowledge itself.

The following prophetic hadith clarifies this reality plainly, wherein the noble Prophet *(s)* mentions: '*During the journey in which Moses (a) and Khidr (a) witnessed strange events, a sparrow appeared and sitting upon the edge of the boat, dipped its beak once or twice in the ocean. So Khidr (a) observed, "O Moses, my knowledge and your knowledge would not decrease from Allah's knowledge what this sparrow has decreased from the ocean!"* [17]

Just like the knowledge of a small ant is considered to be almost nothing when compared to the knowledge and intelligence of humans, likewise our state is considered negligible in relation to Allah (swt). And whatever man knows from all sciences and matters is seen as nothing when compared to what he does not know. This is from amongst the reasons Allah (swt) describes humans as ignorant in the noble Quran, a characteristic that is primary and inherent within us.

In contrast, Allah (swt) explains the greatness of divine knowledge and its limitless nature by His Words: **"And if all the trees on earth were pens, and if the sea and seven more added to it [were ink], the Words of Allah would not be exhausted! Truly, Allah is Mighty, Wise."** [18]

There are many and more divine wisdoms and secrets which the limited, human mind is incapable of grasping as the knowledge of all creations in the universe doesn't even equal a drop from the ocean compared to the knowledge of Allah (swt). Small portions of these secrets have been uncovered to the choicest of the choicest of Allah's (swt) slaves and to a greater degree to the Prophets and by the greatest degree to our noble Prophet *(s)*. Hence the Prophet *(s)* mentions: *"If you knew what I know you would laugh little and weep aplenty"* [19]

To sum up, our elevated, Islamic religion should be taken from the scholars and *arifeen* that have *taqwa*, excellent manners and morals, righteous deeds and live their lives in accordance with the Quran and *Sunnah*. Holding fast to the Quran and Sunnah and abiding by them with consistency is considered amongst the greatest *karamaat* (miracles) of our time.

Indeed, the case of *Abu Yazid al-Bistami* (r), one of the great 'people of truth', is considered a typical example in revealing whether someone is worthy of consideration in the field of religion or not:

One day *Abu Yazid al-Bistami* (r), went out with one of his disciples *(mureed)* to visit a man who had made himself famous with (the claim of) friendship with Allah (swt) (*wilayah*). The man was sought-out for and famous for his abstinence. So, they proceeded until they reached his home. However, when the man exited and entered the masjid, he spat in the direction of the *qiblah* (of Mecca). So, *Abu Yazid al-Bistami (r)* took off without even greeting him and said, '*This one is not trustworthy over the etiquettes of the Messenger (s) of Allah* (swt). *So how could he be trustworthy over what is claimed of him (from the secrets of Allah* (swt))?'

Al-Imam al-Rabbani (r), says:

'*One shouldn't be complacent in the performance of recommendable actions (mustahab), for they are beloved to Allah* (swt). *If one action is agreeable and beloved to Allah and made easy to perform with its requisites, one should benefit from it. It is like buying priceless jewels with pieces of pottery!*'

Once al-Imam al-Rabbani (r) said to one of his students:

'*Bring us some cloves from the garden.*' The student proceeded to the garden and brought 6 cloves with him. When the

Imam saw this in his student's hand, signs of regret and worry became apparent on his countenance and he remarked,

"Our students have continued to not observe the hadith of the Prophet (s) when he said – Indeed Allah is witr (an odd number i.e. One) and loves the witr (odd numbers)[20] – and observance of the odd is from the recommended actions (mustahabbat)." [21]

What do people consider about the recommended actions (mustahab)?

The *mustahab* are beloved to Allah (swt). So, if the entire world and hereafter were spent in exchange for a deed that Allah (swt) loves, it is as if nothing has been spent. We should observe the mustahab to the degree that when we wash our faces, we take great care that the water strikes the right cheek before the left. That is because starting with the right side in actions is from the *mustahab*.

As it has been clarified earlier, the most supreme miracle (*kiramaa*) of the scholars and arifeen, who appreciated the Messenger*(s)* like he deserved to be, was their steadfastness in accurately and precisely following the honourable, prophetic sunnah in action and repose, and in all states, great and small.

Let us also not forget that Allah (swt) has hidden from us the extent of His Pleasure and His Wrath emerging from our deeds. Since we don't know from which of our deeds Allah's (swt) Pleasure or Fury is manifested, we should be taking great care on performing every righteous deed and distancing ourselves from every sin and fault. For the Pleasure of Allah (swt) and likewise His Anger, are sometimes expressed in a great action, sometimes in a mediocre action and at times, even in what we deem as an extremely minor action.

It appears in one of the noble *hadith*, that Allah (swt) had forgiven a prostitute all her sins and made her one of the people of paradise for merely giving water to a thirsty dog, saving it from death. In contrast, it also appears in another *hadith* that Allah (swt) made a woman from amongst the denizens of hell because of her oppression to a cat. She had been the reason for its death when she had locked it up, didn't feed it nor let it free to scavenge on the face of the earth, until it died.

The great companion, *Anas bin Malik* (r) mentioned:

'*You all deem a deed as being more insignificant than a hair, whereas we would consider it, in the time of the Prophet(s), as amongst the (spiritually) destructive sins.*'

The companions, because of the love and great fear in their hearts towards Allah (swt), would deem even small sins as great loss and disobedience – even a cause for spiritual destruction. That is because, they wouldn't look at the size of the sin, but rather would consider the Greatness of Allah (swt) – the One whose order has been disobeyed.

And so, it can be concluded, that it is not enough for someone to be a perfect believer by just performing the compulsory *(fard)* actions and avoiding the forbidden ones. One's faculty and sensitivity of the (spiritual) heart should be filled and overflowing with the implications and nuances of true belief.

In regard to this matter *Shaykh Musa Tuvash Effendi* (r) stated:

"Many people believe that they can perform what is necessary and obligated upon them from religious duties such as prayer, fasting of Ramadan etc. and then relax with peace of mind. However, this is not sufficient. It is also necessary from the point of respect and honouring the orders of Allah (swt), that one be graced with kindness towards Allah's (swt) creatures. And this is not achieved, except with self-sacrifice and sincere, truthful service to others. So the matter that every Muslim of sound mind should attend to and have concern for, after performing compulsory actions and refraining from forbidden ones, is service to Islam, society and all creatures and working towards changing oneself to become a pro-active and beneficial element in society... This perfects and complements the necessary (fard) actions and are taken from the sunnah of our Prophet(s)..."

Finally, how great is this beautiful prayer and supplication from al-Imam al-Rabbani (r):

"O Allah...save us from external speech that is without truthful, complementary (spiritual) states and from knowledge without action – by the sacredness of the master of men (Muhammad), who was sent to all nations – whether they be dark, brown or white! May the best of prayers and most perfect salutations be upon him and his family!" – Ameen.

Footnotes

1. Quran; 4:80.
2. Quran; 3:31.
3. Such as Lent in Catholicism.
4. The Muslims of the sunnah and the community; the saved sect.
5. There is nothing more astonishing about a miracle, then there is the earth's orbit around the sun, the growth of fruits, the bearing of children, the fall of rain and all causes in our universe. For these are all miracles of Allah's *(swt)* power, knowledge and will. The only difference being we have grown accustomed to these latter 'miracles' and deem them 'ordinary'.
6. The Islamic, legal process in which a qualified scholar (*mujtahid*) resorts to the Islamic sources of law to derive a legal ruling for a new matter in which there is no former legal precedent.
7. *Riwaya* and *sanad*; referring to the major methods employed by Muslims to safeguard the hadith and the Quran among generations. Chains of narrations are recorded detailing who heard what and going back all the way to the Prophet *(s)*. Each narrator generally also has something of a character reference, detailing

who they are, how reliable they are, any character defects and the strength of their memories.
8. Sunan Abu Dawud, Hadith number 4604. Book 42, Hadith 9.
9. Sunan Abu Dawud, hadith number 3050. Book 20, Hadith 123.
10. Quran; 26:193-195
11. Quran; 2:2.
12. Quran; 52:7-8
13. Ibn Rajab al-Hanbali, Al-Takweef min al-Naar, Damascus 1979. Pg. 30. (Arabic reference)
14. The highest level of Islamic legal scholars, who are qualified to extract new rulings from the Islamic sources of law; those that are qualified to perform *ijtihad*.
15. The generation immediately following the Companions (Sahabah) of the Prophet.
16. Quran 35:28
17. Sahih Bukhari, Book 3, Hadith 64.
18. Quran; 31:27
19. Sahih Bukhari, Book 83, Hadith 11.
20. Sunan Abi Dawud, Book 8, Hadith 1.
21. The Imam was admonishing his student for not bringing an odd number of cloves. Showing the degree to which he would honour and observe the sunnah of the noble Prophet (s).

CHAPTER 3

Wisdoms from Imam Rabbani - Part 2

If we could revive the captivation of the blessed month of Ramadan to the rest of the days of the year in accordance with the saying – "Act as if everyone you see is Khidr[1] (a) and that every night is the Night of Power[2] (laylat ul-qadr)" – then all of our lives would be full, with the permission of Allah, with brilliance and spiritual excellence and be turned into a month of Ramadan whose nights are spent with taqwa (God-consciousness/piety) and turn the moment of our last breath into a night of ecstasy.

Al-Imam al-Rabbani (r) says:
"*Virtue is dependent on following the noble sunnah of the Prophet(s), and excellence is coupled with reviving and implementing the shariah (Islamic law) which he came with. For example, sleeping after zuhur (the mid-day prayer) in accordance*

with the prophetic sunnah is superior than spending a thousand nights without observing it... and giving a seed in zakat (compulsory charity) in accordance with the Lawgiver's commands (i.e. Allah(swt)) is better than spending a mountain of gold out of one's own accord."

Truly, the responsibility of the believer (*mu'min*) is implementing the orders of Allah(swt) simply because Allah (swt) has ordered him to do so – in the form and manner that the Messenger*(s)* applied. Action in this domain according to one's opinion takes one out of the prophetic sunnah – even if it is with good intention – and drives him to fall into error. Hence it is necessary to learn the requested, righteous actions from the sunnah to implement them, as well as their timings, their methods, their significance and their forms.

In as much so the Prophet*(s)* said:

"Small deeds according to the sunnah are better than many in innovation and he who follows me is from me and he who turns away from my way is not from me"

The following incident elucidates this reality clearly:

One day *Saeed ibn al-Museeb (r)* – one of the great scholars of the *tabieen* (successors of the *sahabah*) – saw a man pray 2 cycles (*rak'aat*) after the *asr* prayer. *Saeed ibn al-Museeb (r)* was not pleased with the action of this man since his prayer fell in a time in which prayer is disliked[3]. The man retorted to argue for his mistake, "O Imam! Would Allah (swt) chastise me for praying?"

The Imam replied, *"No! But He will chastise you for opposition to the sunnah!"*[4]

Fudayl ibn Iyyad [5] (r) says regarding this matter:

"*Truly, if actions are sincere yet **not proper**, they are not accepted. And if they are proper yet **not sincere**, they are not accepted. Only when they are **both sincere and proper**, are they accepted. Their sincerity is that they be (purely) for Allah (swt) and their properness is that they be according to the sunnah.*"

Based upon this, if we want our deeds to be performed for the good pleasure of Allah (swt), it is necessary that we strive for sincerity of intention in our hearts and conformity to the *sunnah* in our actions.

So, for example, the Prophet*(s)* advised us with a particular and fixed litany *(wird)* after the compulsory prayers and that is repeating *subhanAllah* (Glorified is Allah) 33 times, *alhamdulilAllah* (The Praise is Allah's) 33 times and *Allahu Akhbar* (Allah is the Greatest) 33 times. It is not appropriate that we increase this fixed number such as to repeat them 34 times under the pretext of seeking increased reward. Actions like these are not from *taqwa* (piety), on the contrary, they are considered a great affront to the counsel of the Messenger*(s)* with the introduction of our opinion into it. Allah (swt) says in the noble Quran:

"**O you who believe! Advance not before God and His Messenger...**"[6]

Thinking that our own opinions and personal standards are more correct than the clear instructions in the Book and the sunnah in a particular matter is from the most atrocious types of heedlessness and misguidance.

Once a man came to the renowned *Imam, Malik ibn Anas (r)* and asked him, 'O Imam, from whence should I begin the *ihram*[7]?'

He said, "*From Dhul Hulaifah, where the Prophet(s) began the ihram. That is what is in accordance with the sunnah.*"

Except that the man replied, "I wish to begin the *ihram* from the Prophet's(s) masjid (in Medina)".

Said the Imam, "Don't do so."

"I want to begin the ihram from the Prophet's masjid near his blessed grave," he insisted.

The Imam *(r)* replied, "*Don't do so. I fear you falling into fitna (strife, trial).*"

"And what *fitna* is there in this? It is just a distance that I have increased!"

"*And which fitna is greater than you seeing yourself make longer what the Messenger(s) of Allah (swt) shortened!? Indeed, I have heard the word of Allah (swt)-* '**...So let those who contradict his command be wary, lest a trial befall them, or a painful punishment befall them**'[8]."

As it is made clear in what was presented, excessiveness and surpassing limits, even in righteous deeds, should be avoided. The opinion that excessiveness in worship is considered a form of devoutness and *taqwa* is not appropriate.

The Prophet(s) had once forbidden a companion who was acting in this zealous and excessive manner and wanted to fast every day of the year. The Prophet(s) forbade him from such and when the companion insisted on his desire, the Prophet(s) advised him on fasting the fast of Prophet David (*a*) as the limit. This was fasting one day and not the next. Afterwards, when the companion advanced in years and even the fast of Prophet David (*a*) became burdensome on him, he would voice his regret on not following the concession the Prophet(s) was advising him with, in his younger days.

Just as the excessiveness of a believer in his righteous actions due to his personal ideas is considered an error, likewise, minimising and decreasing them, in the same way is also an error.

If we consider the counsel of the Prophet (s) in the matter of the number of glorifications *(tasbihaat)* after the compulsory prayers, which are set as 33 times, and were we to say, '32 times is enough' – then we would do well to remember what occurred with Prophet *Younus* (Jonah) (*a*) in this regard:

Our master Younus (*a*) was commanded with remaining with his people 40 days to convey to them the divine message. However, at the end of 37 days he became fed up with his people who didn't respond or believe in his message. So, he left delivering the message while three days still remained to be completed from the term commanded by Allah (swt). Prophet *Younus* (*a*) stricken with despair and hopelessness in his people left the town. It was later, when having to face with the frightening events of the ship which he was upon, did he understand the gravity of his mistake, except he was thrown into the sea. And as he was rebuking himself and regret overwhelmed him over his mistake, a giant whale swallowed him whole. The Prophet *Younus* (*a*) repented to his Lord and pleaded for His Forgiveness and busied himself with remembrance and glorification while in the belly of the beast.

Allah (swt) explains his condition in these Quranic verses:

"And [remember] Dhu'l-Nun, when he went away in anger, and thought We had no power over him. Then he cried out in the darkness, 'There is no god but Thee! Glory be to Thee! Truly I have been among the wrong-doers'"[9]

"And had he not been among those who glorify (Allah), he would have tarried in its belly till the Day they are resurrected."[10]

Hence, obedience to the orders of Allah (swt) with resoluteness and complete patience is what is required from us. Allah (swt) directs another admonishment citing Prophet Younus (*a*) as an example:

"So be patient with thy Lord's Judgment and be not like the companion of the fish, who cried out while choking with anguish. Had not the blessing from his Lord reached him, he would surely have been cast upon the barren shore still blameworthy."[11]

As it can be seen from the above, servitude (to God) is tied to being able to correctly perform the divine commandments as they appear – without increase or decrease. As the goal of righteous deeds isn't the deeds themselves, rather the goal is submission (to the divine commandment), and love and attachment with Allah (swt) and His Messenger(s). Hence, Allah (swt) has ordered us to obey His Messenger(s) with complete submission:

'O You who believe! Respond to Allah and the Messenger when he calls you unto that which will give you life. And know that Allah comes between a man and his heart..."¹²

Imam Ali (r) expressed the high station of attachment in his heart for the Prophet(s) with beautiful expressions such as, '*You cannot follow anything better than the way of your Prophet(s)*' and '*We had seen the Messenger(s) of Allah (swt) stand, so we stand. We saw him sit, so we sit.*'

The noble companions were lovers of the Prophet(s) and would obey his orders with complete submission, whether they knew the inherent wisdom within those commands or not. One of these lovers was *Abdullah ibn Umar (r)*, who once saw the Prophet(s) drinking from a spring. So, he began going to the same spring and drinking from it every now and then. Another time, he saw the Prophet(s) seeking shade under a certain tree. So, he began seeking the shade of the same tree every now and again. Another time, he saw the Prophet(s) resting his blessed back on a rock while sitting. And so, *Abdullah ibn Umar (r)* also began passing by the same spot and would sit a while resting his back on the same stone. He would say about the wisdom of these actions of his, '*We just do what we saw the Messenger(s) of Allah (swt) do.*'

As for us, we should take the noble companions as a model and example. And be extremely careful not to fall into one of the most widespread errors which so many people have fallen into in our time, which is the sickness of being careless of the *Sunnah*.

Has not Allah said about the Prophet(s), (You truly are) **'upon a straight path'**¹³. Hence, that straightest path for us too, is to exert every possible effort to imitate the Prophet(s) and travel on his illuminated way and holding fast to it like a shadow holds on to its companion.

Let us relate in this regard, the case of one of the most excellent companions, *Uthman ibn Affan (r)*. He was at the utmost levels of submission, truthfulness and sincerity to the Prophet(s). The Messenger(s) had sent *Uthman (r)* as an emissary to the pagans of Mecca before the ratification of the treaty of *Hudaibiyah*. This was to notify them of the intentions of the Muslims in approaching Mecca (from Medina) – that their intention was only to perform the *umrah*. However, the pagans refused entry into Mecca to the Prophet(s) and Muslims with him. On top of that, they held *Uthman (r)* up and said to him – if you want, then you (alone) can make *tawaf* (circumambulation) around the *ka'bah*.

All the Muslims were yearning to perform the *tawaf* and had put the *ka'bah* in their sights. Some of them imagined that *Uthman (r)* had performed the tawaf alone and felt some resentment at that fact. However, that blessed companion, who would ransom himself for the Messenger, delivered an excellent and unrivalled example in sincerity and truthfulness when he replied to the pagans – '*Who am I to do so until the Prophet(s) performs tawaf! I swear by the One, Who in Whose hand is my soul! If I remained here for a year and the Messenger of Allah remained camped at Hudaibiyah, I would not perform tawaf until the Messenger performed tawaf!*'

Despite the burning in the heart of *Uthman (r)* with the fire of yearning towards the ka'bah, he prevented himself from tawaf because of the strength of his spiritual connection with the Prophet(s) and his sincerity towards him. He was ashamed to advance before the Prophet(s) – even in an act of worship.

This was because the sincerity of that eminent companion towards the Messenger(s) of Allah (swt), as well as submission and love for him, all necessitated this honourable station. He shed light on the hadith of the Prophet(s) – *'A man is with whom he loves'* – and embodied it while on the ground of this world in a peerless manner.

So here we witness true love. It is a connection between two hearts. It is the ability to live with the same heart although in different bodies. And to exchange the sensitivities and feelings of that same heart.

This love on both sides can be seen when the rumour of the martyrdom of *Uthman (r)* reached the Muslims at *Hudaibiyah*, the Prophet(s) met the sincerity of *Uthman (r)* with love and friendship in an even more beautiful and excellent way. That was when he took the pledge from all the companions to fight the pagans if the situation required so. The Prophet gestured his right hand and said – *'This is Uthman's hand'* – and joining it with his left hand said – *'This is for Uthman'*. Thereby expressing his love and regard for him. Thankfully, it was not long until the pagans sent a messenger to ratify the treaty of *Hudaibiyah* and *Uthman (r)* returned safe and sound soon after.

Accordingly, what draws the good pleasure of Allah (swt) and love from the Messenger(s) is the sincerity, love, submission and obedience the servant carries in his heart. Nothing can fill the empty space which occurs at the absence or deficiency of these matters. Hence, observance of the commands of Allah (swt) and His Messenger(s) requires great attention. It also demands action with complete foresight and with the wisdom to be able to select the more important action or thing over what is less important. And that too is in accordance with what the conditions and circumstances require.

In this regard, we narrate an incident which occurred with one of the eminent companions, *Abdullah ibn Rawahah (r)*. And the admonition of the Prophet (s) to him, as it carries an important evidence to what we are discussing.

The Prophet (s) once sent out *Abdullah ibn Rawahah (r)* with a group and this happened to fall on a Friday. His companions set out early morning, as for him, he said to himself – I will remain behind to pray with the Prophet (s) and then I will catch up with them. When the Prophet (s) saw him after the prayer, he asked him, *'What prevented you from leaving early morning with your companions?'*

He replied, 'I desired to pray with you and then catch up with them.'

To which the Prophet (s) said, *'If you had spent everything on the earth you wouldn't reach the excellence of their setting out in the morning!'*

Abdullah ibn Rawahah (r) was one of the companions who was present at the pledge of *Aqabah*[14]. The Prophet (s) also gave him glad tidings of martyrdom to which he became eager for and eventually achieved in the battle of *Mutah*. He also gave his wealth to the *bait-ul-maal* (treasury) of the Muslims and gave his self to Allah (swt) so that he may soar to the highest paradise. Yet despite this eminent companion enjoying all these honours and an elevated station, the heart of our Prophet (s) was saddened and admonished him merely because of a simple delay to an order of prophethood. Even despite him being of noble intention, as he just wanted to tarry a little longer in the companionship of the Prophet (s).

So, we see the importance of being swift to carry out the commands of Allah (swt) and His Messenger (s), as they appear and without delay – whether you know the wisdom behind them or not. Taking a decision contradictory to or inconsistent with any clear matter that the Prophet (s) commanded – be it even with a good intention – may well bring about great loss, as earlier mentioned.

One should remember that excessive zeal which makes one forget obedience to the command of Allah (swt) as well as excessive etiquette that reaches the point of not following the commands are considered a type of disobedience. When one acts on his own opinion or personal beliefs, then he may be sometimes driven to falling into this type of error while he thinks he is doing what is right. Hence one should never transgress what the Messenger (s) came with, that is one should avoid one's own opinion, i.e. saying 'according to my opinion...' (in matters of religion), when there are clear and detailed judgements in the Islamic texts.

* * *

Al-Imam al-Rabbani (r) says:

"Be serious about the tahajjud prayer! (late night, voluntary prayer). Whoever wants to reach the treasure of that lofty station, that is the station of intercession, then let him perform the tahajjud prayer and never miss it!"

While in the noble Quran it is mentioned:

"And keep vigil in prayer for part of the night, as a supererogatory act for thee. It may be that thy Lord will resurrect thee in a praiseworthy station."[15]

The *tahajjud* prayer was compulsory only for the Prophet (s). As for us, it is an important and stressed (*muakkada*) *sunnah*. Allah (swt) ordered his beloved with tahajjud and spending the last portion of the night just before dawn with reciting the Quran and with *dhikr* (remembrance of Allah (swt)) and in return He gave good tidings of achieving the praiseworthy station (*maqam al-mahmoodah*). The praiseworthy station is the high level of greater intercession for the gathering of resurrection and judgement, a station which all people are joyous of – from the first generations to the last.

The Prophet (s) would guard his *tahajjud* prayer, giving it great and special importance and would never neglect it – whether on a journey or not. He would also advise his noble companions with this act of worship. As is mentioned in one noble hadith – '*The illustrious of my nation are the memorisers of the Quran and the companions of the night (i.e. those that pray in the nights).*'

The Prophet(s) once said to Abdullah ibn Amr ibn al-As (r) as an advice – '*O Abdullah! Don't be like so and so! He used to pray the nights but then left it."*

Another companion, *Amr ibn Abasah* (r) mentions:

I came to the Messenger(s) of Allah (swt) and asked – *O Messenger of Allah! Is there an hour closer to Allah than others?*

To which the Messenger(s) replied, *"Yes, the last part of the night, so pray as much as you want until you pray the subh (Fajr Prayer)".*[16]

Abu Yazid al-Bistami (r), who is considered one of the leaders of the 'people of truth', began his study of the noble Quran and reciting it while he was still quite young. Once while reciting the Quran, he reached the words of Allah (swt):

"O thou enwrapped! Stand vigil at night, save a little,"[17]

So, he said to his father, *"Dear father, who is the one Allah is speaking to here?"*

His father replied, *"Son, that is the Messenger of Allah!"*

Abu Yazid asked, *"Father, why don't you do like the Prophet (s) did?"*

"My son, praying at night was specific to him as opposed to his nation," he replied out of assumption. To which Abu Yazid fell silent and carried on with his recitation of the Quran till he reached the words of Allah (swt):

"Truly thy Lord knows that thou do stand vigil wellnigh two-thirds of the night, or a half of it, or a third of it, as do a group of those who are with thee..."[18]

So, he said, *"O father! I have heard that a group were performing the night prayer, who is this group!?"*

"My son, they are his companions!"

To which Abu Yazid replied, *"Father, what good is there then in leaving what the Prophet (s) did and his companions?"*

"You have said the truth, my son," his father replied, and he began to perform the night prayer after this incident.

One night, Abu Yazid awoke and found his father praying and so he said, *"Father! Teach me how to purify myself and pray with you."*

His father replied, *"Son, go to sleep you are still small!"*

He replied, *"Father, when it is the Day (of Judgement) and men come forward in groups to be shown their deeds, shall I say to my Lord that I asked my father to show me how to purify myself and pray with him but he rejected and told me to go to sleep because I am still small! Would you be pleased with that?"*

"By Allah I would not my son! Rather, I would love this" – and he taught him what he needed to know. And from then on, Abu Yazid (r) would rise at night and pray with his father, while he was still small.

Later, he is known to have said – '*No secrets were made unveiled to me except after I turned my nights into days.*'

When the believer can take advantage of those late-night moments (just before *Fajr*), sticking to the advice of the Prophet (s), worshiping as he did, then one's nights will become brighter than their days. Also, so that the servant can realise the optimal benefit of having his nights filled with spiritual radiance, then it is essential that he carries the spiritual impression he receives in the night to his day and protects himself from committing sin in the daytime.

In this regard, *Ibrahim bin Adham* (r) once said to a man who was suffering from the inability to wake up for the *tahajjud* prayer, '*Don't disobey Allah (swt) in the day and He will let you stand before Him in the night.*'

Hasan al-Basri (r) would say, '*A servant will certainly commit a sin and because of it, the tahajjud prayer will be forbidden for him.*'

Certainly, the desire for worshipping in the night is in accordance to the strength of one's love, in his heart, for Allah (swt). And making one's nights alive with worship and dhikr is a most beautiful expression of one's ardent emotion of love and glorification to their Lord (swt). Hence, the famous expression about worshipping in this time – '*It is not the affair of every Muslim, rather it is only the deed of the very pious.*'

Allah (swt) mentions about His successful, sincere and pious servants, who forsake the warmth of their beds and the sweetness of sleep in the last portion of the night and then engage themselves in His worship and remembrance:

"Truly the reverent shall be amidst gardens and springs, partaking of that which their Lord has given them. Truly they were virtuous aforetime. Little of the night did they slumber, and at dawn would seek forgiveness. And in their wealth was a due for the beggar and the deprived."[19]

The blessed nights of Ramadan are also considered a means to achieve the virtue of night worship. They are like yearly exercises that Allah (swt) has blessed us with so that we may be accustomed to praying at night. Ramadan is considered as a peerless opportunity for spiritual gain as it contains within it

Laytul-Qadr (the Night of Decree), in which the excellence of worship therein is equal to one thousand ordinary months. This blessed night is unique to the ummah of our master, Muhammad (s).

It is therefore upon us, to extend the virtue of worshipping in the blessed nights of Ramadan to all the days of the year in accordance to the saying – *"Act as if everyone you see is Khidr (a) and that every night is the Night of Power (Laytul-Qadr)"* – then all of our lives would be full, with the permission of Allah (swt), with brilliance and spiritual radiance and be turned into a month of Ramadan whose nights are spent with taqwa (God-consciousness/piety) and turn the moment of our last breath into a night of ecstasy.

We ask Allah (swt), Most High, All Powerful that He doesn't let us leave Ramadan, but He purifies us from our sins and transgressions – from His Kindness and Generosity. And that He blesses us with a life overflowing with spirituality and with the ambience of Ramadan. And that He makes our last breath peaceful and calm like the tranquillity of the morning of Eid, opening up to eternal happiness. Ameen!

Footnotes

1. Khidr (a) is a central character in tassawuf. He is mentioned in the Quran as a temporary guide to Moses (a). It is said he still interacts with and aids Allah's (swt) special servants with His Permission.
2. A hidden night said to occur in the last 10 nights of Ramadan, but whose exact date is unknown. It is known to be better than a thousand months as worship in it equates to worshipping continuously for a thousand months. And Allah knows best.
3. i.e. after the *asr* prayer until the *maghrib* prayer. Prayer is disliked in this time period.
4. Chastisement here may not necessary be punishment in the hereafter, but could also be loss of spiritual rank, loss of spiritual blessings like wisdom, knowledge, humility, loss of strength or desire to perform good deeds, or being left alone to be over-powered by one's nafs or *shaytan* etc...And Allah *(swt)* knows best.
5. He *(r)* was amongst the great ascetics and scholars of the early Muslim generations. He was once a highway robber who renounced his ways to such an extent he was later known as *Abid al-Haramayn*, the Worship-

per of the Two Muslim Sanctuaries, i.e. Mecca and Medina. For not a spot of the two masjids remained where his tears did not fall.
6. Quran; 49:1. Commentary: "...*More broadly, it indicates that people should not follow their own opinions rather than the teachings of the Prophet or allow personal desires to take precedence over the commands of God and the Prophet*" – The Study Quran, Seyyed Hossein Nasr et.al.
7. The special, prohibiting state a Muslim enters into when performing Hajj or Umrah.
8. Quran; 24:63
9. Quran; 21: 87
10. Quran; 37:143-144
11. Quran; 68:48-49
12. Quran; 8:24
13. Quran; 36:4
14. The Pledge of *Aqabah* occurred when the Ansar of Medina pledged allegiance to the Prophet (s), when he and the early Muslims were still being persecuted in Mecca.
15. Quran; 17:79
16. Sahih Bukhari, Vol.1, Book 5, Hadith 1364.
17. Quran; 73:1-2
18. Quran; 73:20
19. Quran; 51:15-19

CHAPTER 4

Wisdoms from Imam Rabbani - Part 3

Fasting is a beautiful translation of those silent shouts and moans of the oppressed and needy that say – 'Have sympathy...'. If we cannot advance our mercy and compassion over our temporary, worldly desires, then we are oppressing our true nature. We should know that the countries that don't disperse the seeds of compassion on their soil will not save themselves from turning their futures into fields of pains and funerals.

Al-Imam al-Rabbani (r) says:
"*The servant should strive, in all his deeds, actions and even repose, to seek the good-pleasure of Allah and his exterior and his hidden state should be directed to Him and in a state of remembrance of Him.*

For instance, if one desires to sleep – something which is heedlessness through and through – but with the intention to divert weariness so that he may continue in his worship in a more excellent manner, then his sleep will become a source of worship as long as he remains sleeping. As it is as if he is in obedience by having the intention to accomplish his obedience. 'The sleep of the scholars is worship' – as the famous saying goes."

Hence, us humans, who were created for the purpose of worshipping our Lord, should expend as much effort as possible to realise this reality and be conscious of it until the last breath of our lives. The true believer is always seeking the good-pleasure of Allah (swt), every moment of his life. The ideal believer doesn't see any of his deeds as being sufficient but rather yearns to continue increasing in goodness.

Worship of Allah isn't just ritual fulfilled and perfected in defined and specific times like prayer, fasting, *zakat* and *hajj*. Rather worship of Allah (swt) is also, besides this, a system of living that continues the span of one's life and encompasses a believer at every moment. Such as noble manners and interactions with others. Allah's promise to reward extends to all actions that bring about His Good-Pleasure, not just the rituals. Likewise, all actions that induce His Anger are forbidden.

Based on this, the believer must exert his utmost effort to relate all his worldly actions and deeds that are outside the realm of stipulated ritual worship to superior motives like obedience to Allah, so that he may achieve His Good-Pleasure thereby. Imam Rabbani (r) mentions in regard to this:

*"Affluence shouldn't be sought or be noticeable in regard to eating delicious foods or wearing valuable garments. Rather, what is proper in the consumption of foods and drink is to do so with the intention to gain strength to perform worship. As for wearing expensive garments, one should intend to beautify the command of Allah – '**O Children of Adam! Put on your adornment at every place of worship...**'[1] - that is at every prayer. And to not mix one's intention with showing-off in front of people and boastfulness."*

Hence, whenever someone performs even his daily duties and meets his daily needs with a sincere intention for the Good-Pleasure of Allah (swt) then the stamp of worship is imprinted on that action.

Our elevated religion directs believers towards divine matters in order to distance them from the desires of the self. Further, it relates to even material and external matters and makes them spiritual, increasing them with elevated and sublime meanings. The believer is not only elevated because of ritual worship and elevated behaviour but excellency is also attributed to him because of his intentions with even his bodily needs.

Food and drink are considered a need of the body. However, Islam has raised these apparently trivial actions by allowing a person to attain reward and spiritual increase through connecting one's intention of strengthening worship through them. Likewise, beginning eating with *bismallah*, imparts on us meditation of Allah's great bounties and kindnesses with every morsel we take. And afterwards, motivates us to Allah's praise, thankfulness and remembrance. That is, food that is consumed with Allah (swt) in mind and to benefit the body in this regard, beautifies one with spiritual increase and light and hence becomes a type of worship.

This then is our complete Islamic religion, which ties every need of man with elevated goals like in the aforementioned examples and grants us ample opportunities at every moment of our lives to reach Allah's Good-Pleasure.

The food and drink of the believers – whose hearts are spiritually awake and they take advantage of these opportunities – all their movements and non-movements, standing and sitting and even their sleeping, becomes worship due to their sincere intentions. The opposite is also true. Even the worship of the heedless may bring on divine anger because of their mixing personal motives, such as showing off and boasting, into their intentions.

Then, for us to live with every moment being regarded as worship, we should submit our hearts to the nurture and discipline required. We must, in this regard, acquire good and pure intentions. As the Prophet (swt) said, '*The intentions of a believer are better than his actions*'.[2]

Besides this, Allah (swt) offers many righteous deeds to his servants that act with sincerity, so that they may make their lives into continual worship. For example, sometimes the servant is incapable to perform the voluntary deeds he was consistent in because of day to day conditions affecting him – such as sickness, travel, over-weariness or old age. In such circumstances, Allah (swt) offers the continual reward of those actions as if he was consistent in them because of one's sincere intention.

The explainers (*mufassireen*) of the Quran say about the following verse:

"...save those who believe and perform righteous deeds; for theirs shall be a reward unceasing."[3] – that the reward of the slave for bodily actions continues indefinitely even when he becomes unable to perform them. And that is in accordance with what he exhibited out of sincere intention and his exertion to perform the deeds when he was healthy. Hence, we should strive to continue in our worship and righteous deeds while we have the available opportunity.

Truly, the worship of the Prophet (s), who is the greatest and most excellent example we have been honoured with, was dominant in every area of his life with complete control and equilibrium. When his blessed life is observed, it occurs to one that he spent every moment of his life in worship.

The case is that the Prophet (s), besides being constantly devoted to a life of worship to the highest degree, never slackened in his worldly duties either, rather he perfected them. In reality, from one side the Prophet (s) continued performing his worship day and night with complete devotion and carefulness, spread the religion with which Allah (swt) sent him– bearing all kinds of troubles and difficulties on its path, clarified and explained the revelation when needed to his people with his words and actions and on the other side, cared for his family and their affairs, shared in the worries and anxieties of the poor, took part in funerals, laid down the foundations of an unmatched strong and sound political state, sent messengers to kings calling them to Islam, accepted messengers from other kings and travellers taking care of their arrival and stay, travelled with his army and oversaw its management and organisation and fought and made heavy sacrifices in the path of removing the obstacles that prevented the spread of Islam.

None of his worldly responsibilities distracted or prevented him from his worship. On the contrary, the Prophet (s) lived every moment of his life as worship since he performed his worldly responsibilities too with what was good-pleasing to Allah (swt). Besides the great day to day responsibilities on his shoulders that no one else could bear, he still worshiped Allah (swt) more excellently and perfectly than monks who had segregated and renounced the world, confining themselves in temples for worship and devotions.

* * *

Al-Imam al-Rabbani (r) says:

'The performance of one compulsory (fard) prayer in congregation is better than thousands of prayers performed in seclusion away from the congregation (jama'ah). And remembrance (dhikr) and contemplation in a manner that is consistent with the rulings and manners of the Shariah is more excellent and important'.

Islam rejects individualism and rather guides to social life and self-lessness. The first aspect of social training Islam offers are the prayers in congregation. For it is here that the seeds of the sentiments of unity, support and cooperation of the believers are sown, grow and strengthen. The Prophet (s) said,

'Adhere to the Jama'ah (the group of Muslims), beware of separation, for indeed Shaytan is with one (who is alone) and he is further away from the two. Whoever wants the best place in Paradise, then let him stick to the Jama'ah...'[4]

'A man's prayer offered with another man is purer than his prayer which he offers alone, and his prayer with two men is purer than his prayer with one and if they are more (in number), it is more beloved to Allah, the Mighty, the Majestic.'[5]

Once the blind companion, *Abdullah ibn Umm Maktoum* came to the Messenger (s) and said, *'O Messenger of Allah there are many venomous creatures and wild beasts in Madinah (so allow me to pray in my house because I am blind).'*

The Prophet (s) said, 'Do you hear the call of – Come to Prayer! Come to Success! (haya ala salah, haya ala al-falah)? – (if so) then you must come.'[6]

So, see how the Prophet (s), who is the most merciful and compassionate of people, replied to his blind, old companion – so what about those who can see! Deep consideration should be given to the seriousness, extent of loss and frightening ignorance that constitutes opposing the congregation without a valid, legal excuse.

Shifa bint Abdullah (r) narrates, *'...Umar ibn al-Khattab found two men sleeping and said, 'What is it with these two? They weren't present with me in the prayer?'*

I said, 'O Commander of the Believers, they prayed with the people (and it was the month of Ramadan) until the morning, then they prayed the fajr prayer and fell asleep.'

Umar replied, 'That I pray the fajr in congregation is more beloved to me than I pray the entire night.'

There are plenty of actions and duties that are binding on the believer at every moment. What is necessary upon the believer is to give priority to performing the most important duties first and then striving with one's utmost in performing those of lesser importance.

No doubt that what takes precedence are the compulsory actions *(faraid)*. Busying oneself with other matters at the time when the compulsory actions are stipulated is mistaken. Even if those other matters are voluntary good actions or other beneficial deeds.

The compulsory actions in one's religious life, come before all other deeds. The performance of voluntary *(nawafil)* deeds are only performed on top of and after the compulsory one's have been completed. It is mentioned in a *hadith qudsi* [7], that Allah (swt) says,

'...the most beloved thing with which My slave comes nearer to Me is what I have enjoined upon him; and My slave keeps on coming closer to Me through performing nawafil (voluntary deeds) till I love him. And when I love him, I become his hearing with which he hears, his seeing with which he sees, his hand with which he strikes, and his leg with which he walks, and if he asks from Me, I give him, and if he seeks My Protection, I protect him.' [8]

Allah (swt) wants us grow closer to him by regularly performing *nawafil* together with the compulsory actions so that we may, as a result, become slaves that He loves. He makes it clear that there isn't a deed more excellent or beloved than the compulsory deeds regarding reaching this exceptional level of slave hood (becoming beloved to Allah). That is, He teaches us that the compulsory deeds are a necessary condition to guarantee the acceptance of other deeds.

* * *

Al-Imam al-Rabbani (r) says,

'*Know that the heart is close to Allah. Nothing is closer to His Sanctity like the heart is. So, beware of hurting any heart whether it be a believer's or a sinner's. For the One close to it protects it – even if it be the heart of a disobedient one. So, beware of that and beware again! For there is after kufr (disbelief), no sin more of an offence to Allah than harming the heart – since it is the closest thing that reaches Him.*"

The Noble Quran clarifies that Allah is closer to His servant than his jugular vein and that He intervenes between a man and his heart.

Hence it is incumbent that we take extreme interest and concern with the heart which is the place of the Divine Gaze. Imam Shah Naqshband (r) says,

'*There is not a heart except the Gaze of Allah is upon it – whether the owner of that heart realises it or not!*'

With this he draws attention on the one hand, that spiritually reviving the heart will be a means to reach spiritual radiance from the Divine Gaze on that heart. But on the other hand, points to the seriousness of actions which spiritually wound the heart and the detrimental result following from it.

One of the greatest concerns and endeavours of the *awliya* (friends) of Allah is to attain a permanent cure, with the light of Islam and *Imaan* (faith), against heedless and sick hearts which distance one from the divine realities. And to also revive the broken and restless hearts of the believers with compassion and mercy.

* * *

Imam Rabbani (r) says,

'*The month of Ramadan gathers within itself all goodness and blessings. And every blessing and goodness that reaches to anyone throughout the year is only a drop from the ocean of blessings of this great month, whose value is immeasurable. And the state of the community in this month is a cause for the condition of that community for the rest of the days of the year. And division within it is a cause for division throughout the year. So great congratulations on those that pass this blessed month and he is pleased with it. And despair to he who was discontented with it and was prevented from its blessings and competition in good deeds.*'

The month of Ramadan is considered the season of goodness, the spiritual spring for the whole year. It is the time of spiritual radiance and blessings, which has acquired unrivalled value and importance with the honour of the Noble Quran being sent down within it and its containing of *laylat ul-qadr* which is better than a thousand months and with the doors of forgiveness and mercy being opened within it.

The community, in this month of happiness and spiritual elevation, acquires for itself exceptional spiritual profits that are reflected upon the entire year. That is why the proof that our worship was accepted in this blessed month is manifested by the state of our hearts and our steadfastness in deeds in the months that follow Ramadan.

Hence those that gift their hearts to Allah (swt) in this blessed month, and their bodies to worship and spend their time with self-sacrifice and service to others, together with fasting, night prayers *(tarawih)*, recitation of the Noble Quran, remembrance *(dhikr)*, asking for forgiveness *(istigfaar)*, charity, compassion and mercy, continue to reach the blessings of these deeds throughout the whole year.

On the other hand, those that are heedless of this blessed time and distance themselves from this divine mercy remain open to heedlessness and losing out on goodness throughout all days of the year. To the extent that the Prophet says in the noble *hadith*,

'*Truly Jibril (a) appeared to me and said, "Wretched be the one who reaches Ramadan and is not forgiven for it!" I replied, 'Ameen'.*

In another *hadith* it is mentioned,

"Despair to he who reaches Ramadan and is not forgiven in it. And if a man is not forgiven in Ramadan, then when will he be forgiven?" [9]

Therefore, reviving the blessed month of Ramadan is considered an extremely important issue in the sight of knowledgeable believers. *Ma'lee ibn Fadl* mentions,

'Our righteous predecessors would make prayers to Allah for six months that they reach Ramadan, and six months after Ramadan that He accept it from them."

From another point of view, the month of Ramadan is considered, in respect to the fasting person's hunger and weakness, a great spiritual training to understand and realise the conditions of the poor and needy – and in an excellent way. Allah (swt) mentions in his Noble Book: **'...you know them by their mark...'**[10]

That is to urge us to seek out the needy who are shy to ask people and request for help due to their great virtue and self-restraint. And that we become acquainted with their conditions and then strive to help them in accordance with our capabilities. That is that Allah (swt) desires that our hearts acquire elevated sensitivity and feelings of compassion, mercy, generosity and sacrifice.

Ramadan is a school that teaches us that we are responsible for the poor, needy, deprived and wayfarers and that they have rights over us. Let us recall a story that is a great lesson so that we too may account ourselves seriously and conscientiously regarding our responsibilities to the poor, homeless and strangers especially in the month of Ramadan:

Once, the Sultan *Mustapha III* went to the fort of *Shaykh ul-Islam Muhammad Ameen Effendi* for breaking his fast in the blessed month of Ramadan. During their conversation the sultan said, '*Effendi! I wish I could visit your more often, but your fort is extremely far from us*'.

The Shaykh replied, '*It's possible that I find a place closer to you. However, none of the places which I have seen in this area have a kitchen.*'

These words surprised the Sultan and he asked, '*How strange! Isn't food being cooked in those houses!?*'

The Shaykh replied, '*The food for all of them comes from the kitchen of this poor man in front of you – every morning and evening. That is why I do not wish to leave this place.*'

When Ramadan falls on such a sensitive heart and selfless soul, then one becomes one of the most excellent observers of servitude to Allah (swt).

Accordingly, being able to revive Ramadan in a manner that is befitting it and while farewelling it while one is happy with it and being able to reach the Ramadan of the following year without losing the spiritual capital which one earned within it – and further being able to live our whole lives with a spirituality that is in accordance with a 'perpetual Ramadan' – all that is considered a great success after which is more success. Indeed, the true *Eid*, is just a manifestation of this happiness.

Yes, the true *Eid* is for the one who exits Ramadan and can witness divine forgiveness. A blessed Eid and congratulations for sincere servitude presented to Allah (swt).

Eid is the last lesson of Ramadan which is, throughout, a school of knowledge and learning. It is a time of visiting friends and close ones, the sick, orphans, the homeless, the deprived, the oppressed – to investigate their conditions, ease their sufferings and to share in their hunger and sadness. In a nutshell, it is living like brothers in religion as a community.

Eid is a time of worshipping together as a community, complete with helping others and sacrificing while increasing in one's individual worship. It isn't a time of idleness and personal pleasure, like some people spend it with extravagance and vanity like holidays filled with the insanity of excessive wastage and negligence.

Eid is a time to spend with a humble heart, to bring our mind to thoughts of religious brotherhood.

We ask Allah (swt) that he gives us the power to feel the pains and sufferings of our brothers and sisters in religion in the East and the West and all over the world, that He makes our hearts places of mercy that shelters all of them, that He makes it possible for us to heal their wounds whether with material help or prayers. And we ask Him that He shines the sun of happiness of a true *Eid* on our Islamic world, so drowning in pains and calamities in this time...

We implore Allah, the Most High, Most Powerful, Capable of His Will, we ask Him from His Kindness and Generosity, that He not make us leave the month of Ramadan without purifying us from our sins and mistakes and that He blesses us with our whole lives surrounded with the ambience of Ramadan, overflowing with spirituality. And that He makes our last breath peaceful and in tranquillity like the serenity of the morning of *Eid*, opening up into an eternal bliss...Ameen!

Footnotes

1. Quran; 7:31
2. *Al Suyuti, al-Jamia al-Sagheer, 2, 194.*
3. Quran; 95:6
4. Jami at-Tirmidhi, 2165
5. Bulugh al-Maram, Book 2, Hadith 418.
6. Sunan Abu-Dawud, Book 2, Hadith 163.
7. A hadith or saying of the Prophet Muhammad (s) in which he conveys meanings from Allah (swt), but in his own words.
8. Riyad as-Salihin, 95
9. Ibn Abi Shaybah, Al-Musnaf, 2, 270.
10. Quran; 2:273

CHAPTER 5

Wisdoms from Imam Rabbani - Part 4

What is this world compared to the eternity of the Hereafter except like a drop from a great ocean? For if the answer to the question – What is life? – is that it can be reduced in the end to the moisture of wet earth and the dead silence found upon gravestones, then what could be more tragic and bitter than a short, passing life, wasted and exhausted for such a miserable end..?

The late Necip Fazil [1] summarised the part of his life which he spent in heedlessness with his words, "For 30 years my watch ticked over, yet I stood still. I played with paper aeroplanes, and yet I was unaware of the sky [2]..."

Imam Rabbani (r) says,

'What is sought from the creation of mankind is the practicing of prescribed worship. And what is sought out from prescribed worship is the attainment of certainty of faith.'

Allah (swt) says in His Noble Book,

'I did not create jinn and mankind, save to worship Me.'[3]

Abdullah ibn Abbas (r) in his commentary on this verse explains that 'to worship Me' here means 'to **know** Me'. For instance, someone may consider a person in prostration (*sujood*) as just performing an external movement. However, he is at this moment closer to his Lord than any other time and the meaning embedded within his prostration is that the believer places his forehead on the ground with complete humility in the divine court, recognising his own weakness and servitude. It is an expression of his submission and resignation in front of his Lord and his knowing Him in his own heart saying – You are my Lord, I am your slave. You are my Creator and I am your creation.

The companions (r) of the Prophet (s) would raise their heads to the sky in their prayers – that is, up until Allah (swt) sent down the verse,

'Truly the believers have prospered, who are humble in their prayers.'[4]

After the revelation of this verse, the noble companions (r) began to bow their heads towards the earth with much humility. This is because they had plunged and delved deeply into the reality of prayer, reaching deep understandings, their worship being performed with complete comprehension of their weakness and poverty in front of Divine Greatness and Power.

So, the goal of worship and servitude is attaining knowledge of Allah (swt) with such awareness and spiritual insight. It is arriving at certainty of faith and understanding its true implications far from doubts and suspicions. It is living with an assured heart at the level of *ihsan* – that is certain conviction that Allah (swt) is as if in front of our very eyes. It is changing the reality of our being, in which every moment is under the Sight and Observance of Divine Omnipotence, so that we grasp this sensitivity in our hearts.

Regarding the believer who truly knows His Lord, he has no other purpose in his life greater than servitude, nor any status higher than the status of servitude. The Prophet (s) was given the choice to be either a prophet-king or a prophet-slave and he chose to be a prophet and a slave.

He (s) signalled through this that the kingdom and rank and happiness that servitude to Allah (swt) brings is greater and more important and more lasting than worldly kingdoms. The happiness from worldly ranks and kingdoms are not even at a level to be compared.

What benefit is there if the entire world was given to someone even for a thousand years? Isn't the place in which he will soon find refuge in, at the end of his road, equivalent to a dark hole in the ground? The life of this world cannot be compared to the eternal life of the hereafter except maybe like a drop in a great ocean.

Therefore, if the answer to the question – What is life? – is that it can be reduced in the end to the moisture of wet earth and the dead silence found upon gravestones, then what could be more tragic and bitter than a short, passing life, wasted and exhausted for such a miserable end?

Allah (swt) says in His Noble Book,

'The Day they see it, it will be as if they had tarried (in this world) but an evening or the morning thereof.'[5]

Hence, there is nothing more rational than making this short life the capital investment of eternal happiness. The way to this is to keep to servitude to Allah (swt) like we have been ordered. The wise scholars of the past advised us this with the phrase, *'The world is but an hour – so let it be in obedience (to Allah)'*.

Shaykh Abdullah al-Dehlawi (r) advised us of the necessity of living our short lives in a state of contentment, training our egos *(nafs)*, keeping far from the forbidden and from doubts and that we concentrate, with all our effort, on our servitude to Allah (swt). He says, *'What is the life of this world, except a day? So let it be a day of fasting.'*

Further, every worshipful act when performed correctly, is considered food for the soul that brings the servant closer to His Lord, strengthens his faith, purifies his heart from uncertainties and doubts and then forwards to him serenity and true tranquillity.

Faith resembles a spring from which light flows. While desires and selfish urges from one's self as well as from satan, are always lurking in the shadows throughout one's life to turn off this light. While worship is like a glass lantern which protects the light of faith against these violent storms.

Whenever truthfulness and sincerity in worship increases, with its manner being sound (i.e. on the way of the Prophet (s)), so too does the light of faith strengthen and glow in the heart.

Sami Effendi clarifies this spiritual state of the believers who reach, through the blessing and bounty of worship and obedience, firm belief which doesn't budge nor wobble. He gives the following comparison:

It is incumbent on the believer that he be truly steadfast and firm like a mountain. A mountain has 4 good qualities, namely:

1. It doesn't melt with the heat.
2. Neither does it freeze with the cold.
3. Nor is it overturned by the wind.
4. And neither is it drifted away by flood.
   The steadfast believer safeguards his faith despite any difficult or negative conditions.

* * *

Imam al-Rabbani (r) says:

'*There can be no deceiving in love. For the lover is fascinated and infatuated with the beloved. He cannot tolerate disagreement with the beloved nor even be inclined to those who go against his beloved in any way.*'

Faith in Allah (swt) is love within the heart. And love is an action of the heart. There is choice with every member of the body except the heart. For nothing can make someone love another forcibly. And likewise, nothing can make one hate another forcibly and under compulsion.

Therefore, the true believer safeguards his heart, the place and headquarters of faith *(imaan)*, from everything that Allah (swt) doesn't like. And neither does he incline his heart towards it. That is because one's claim of loving Allah (swt), yet at the same time inclining towards what Allah (swt) doesn't love doesn't correspond to true faith. The Prophet (s) said, '*A man is with whom he loves*'[6].

So, we must think carefully as to what degree our hearts are attached to Allah (swt). And to what degree are they attached to the Messenger (s). And to what degree are our hearts attached to what Allah (swt) and His Messenger (s) love? And on the other hand, to what degree are our hearts attached to desires and selfish inclinations? And to what degree are they attached to the enemies of Allah (swt) and His Messenger (s), or to the temptations of sins or to the plots of satan?

In true love, the lover loves what the beloved loves and dislikes what the beloved dislikes. So, the lover of Allah (swt) and His Messenger (s) loves praiseworthy, beautiful characteristics like generosity, good manners, modesty, kindness, mercy and forgiveness. On the other hand, he dislikes repugnant, blameworthy characteristics such as insolence, brutality, stinginess, oppression and transgression. That is because true love stems from the common matters between the beloved and loved.

Also, in true love, the characteristics of the beloved flow into the lover, with the love increasing with the emergence of the characteristics of the beloved in the lover.

An example of this is *Abu Bakr as Siddeeq* (r), who was the one to whom most of the manners of the Messenger (s) affected. That is because he was the greatest in love and greatest in annihilation *(fana)*[7] with the Messenger (s). When we look at *Abu Bakr as Siddeeq* (r) it is as if we witness the character of the Messenger (s).

That is to say, the matter doesn't end with merely saying, "I love Allah and His Messenger'. For if we truly love then we should ask ourselves; What is the extent of my compassion? My kindness? At what level is my good character? To what extent are the characteristics of the Messenger (s) existent in me? Am I able to rid myself of selfishness and egotism? Do I care about the worries of the *ummah* (Muslim nation)? Is my soul one of benevolence? Do I reflect my love in my internal states and actions? Or is my love hollow pretence that doesn't exceed the limits of speech!?

Likewise, it is not enough to say – 'I love the Quran'. Rather we should always be increasing in questioning ourselves regarding the Quran. Such as to what level does Quranic character flow into me? To what standard do my deeds level up with the rules of the Quran? Do we send our children to the schools for learning the Noble Quran? To what extent do we help them achieve Quranic morals and characteristics? How much do we think about the position of the Noble Quran over us on the Day of Judgement? Shall it be an intercessor for us or because of our ignoring it, will it be an adversary...?

The measure of true love is, in fact, sacrifice. Empty words whose truthfulness haven't been proven with sacrifice have no meaning or significance at all. *Maulana Jalal al-deen al Rumi* (r) warns the heedless who claim love yet in reality are amongst the furthest away from it: *'(Save your words)...don't become the butt of the joke'*.

When someone who loves his country distances himself from it even a little, he begins to feel a yearning for its air, its water and earth. Even if that land was a barren desert, he would still yearn for it and would hold in his heart an attachment to everything that reminds him of his homeland. This is a sign of true love.

One day *Majnoon*[8] was wandering aimlessly in the wild and in the deserts out of his intense passion and longing for *Leila*. Suddenly he chanced upon a poor, weakly dog whose hair had fallen off and had saliva dripping from its mouth. Yet *Majnoon* began patting it and kissing its forehead. When people saw him in such a state, they began severely criticising and condemning him for his interest and excessive consideration for this tramp of a dog. He replied to them, *'Ahh...if only you saw him with my eyes...you would certainly then know the reason for my actions and approve of me. This is a dog of the neighbourhood of Leila, how often it has gone off to that neighbourhood! And settled down on paths near to Leila! And protected her throughout the night! How can I not love it!'*

In short, everything that Allah (swt) and His Messenger (s) love should be reflected in our states and actions. That is why the people close to Allah (swt) feel a spiritual pleasure and delight that defies description in their following of the Quran and Sunnah. And that too with every matter of their lives, from their food and drink to their standing and sitting.

Further, one of the requirements of true love is that we love what the beloved loves and dislike what the beloved dislikes. Hence, if we truly love Allah (swt) and His Messenger (s), then we should make love for Allah's sake and dislike for Allah's sake as one of the foundational and basic characteristics of our personality. We should love those who are worthy of love and dislike those who are not worthy of it, that is those enemies of Allah (swt) and His Messenger (s), and of Islam and the Muslims.

Allah's rebuke of *Abu Lahab* in *Surah Masad* of the Quran, because of his unrelenting persistence on disbelief, despite his being an uncle of the Prophet (s), is a stark example of this reality.

Hence, we should stop ourselves from praising the enemies of Allah (swt) and His Messenger (s), even from giving them the slightest importance. For such regard offers them greater honour and thus would be a reason to draw the Anger of Allah (swt).

The following hadith is a clear example on the necessary position to take regarding aversion for the sake of Allah (swt): "*Do not address a hypocrite with the title of 'sayyid' (master), for (even) if he is a sayyid, you will displease your Lord, Most High.*[9] (And what then, if he is not a sayyid?).

* * *

Imam al-Rabbani (r) says:

'O lover (of Allah)! Have no grief as long as carelessness over 2 things doesn't occur. The first is the following of the Sunnah of the Prophet (s). The second being sincerity and love for one's shaykh. If thousands of darknesses occur but you have these two, there is no harm or fear of loss. But if – God forbid – there is decrease in one of these matters, then it is loss upon loss. Even so if a man is in hudhoor (a spiritual state) and a state of dhikr (remembrance). One must continually plead & supplicate to Allah (swt) with humility for these two matters and for steadfastness on their paths. For they are the essence of the matter and the point of deliverance.'

The believer must exert his maximum effort in travelling on the way of the Prophet (s) and his inheritors who are the knowers of Allah (*arifeen*) and the scholars. For if he abides to this path, he shall traverse the darkest of roads with safety and reach the door of eternal happiness. On the other hand, the one who travels without a guide and without evidence is like a ship that loses its steering wheel. It goes wherever the wind drives it and moves as the wind moves and yet still doesn't find its path. And further, it won't save itself from destruction and being lost in unknown mazes.

A believer should never think highly of himself nor think that his actions are accepted. Rather he should examine his condition continually and check if he is remaining steadfast and attempt to correct his mistakes. This 'mirror' of steadfastness which shows man his mistakes so that he may correct them is like the Prophet (s) who is considered a living, walking explanation *(tafsir)* of the Noble Quran. As well as his inheritors from the complete spiritual guides – the scholars who act on their knowledge – who are extremely observant and concerned about walking on the bright path of the Prophet (s), without wandering about like an ant.

Just like a sick patient cannot treat his own illness nor diagnose it by reading the books of medicine, likewise it is not in the capability of anyone to correct himself by himself merely by the reading of books. He won't be able to rid himself of his spiritual diseases like conceit, arrogance and boastfulness. Even doctors, when they are struck by disease seek help from other doctors and submit themselves to their care. Likewise, a judge cannot pass judgement on a personal matter for himself, rather he must present himself in front of another judge. This is the reason it is necessary to follow an arrived guide and journeying under his guidance to reach a state of spiritual perfection.

Maulana Jalaluddin Al-Rumi (r) emphasises the importance of submission to the spiritual training at the hands of an arrived guide who is an inheritor of the Prophet (s). That is so one may surpass the obstacles of the self *(nafs)* and arrive at realities and knowledge of Allah *(ma'rifa)*. He says, '*A knife cannot trim its own wooden handle but requires another knife.*

So, you too, O (spiritually) wounded one, go and present your wounds to a surgeon of hearts. For you cannot treat yourself...you know the healthiness of your bodily and mental health from the doctor and you know the soundness of your spiritual state and knowledge, which elevates one to eternity, from an arrived (spiritual) guide.'

The Prophet (s) said - '*The believer is the mirror to the believer*'. And so purified guides are clear and brilliant mirrors for us in which our souls witness their true reality. Those deprived of such mirrors cannot stop their mistakes or notice them just as they can't awaken from the heedlessness of imagining the misery that they suffer from as being happiness.

On the other hand, some ignorant ones who have fallen into such a pit of heedlessness reveal much about their own shortcomings in truthfulness, sincerity, respect and submission to the Prophet (s) through their disregard with his sayings and ways (*sunnah*). Likewise, such wretches insult, insolently and shamelessly, the great saints *(awliya)* on the method of the Prophet (s). As if they themselves have reached the spiritual stations that entitles them to rate and criticise them. No doubt, this is an awful blindness of the heart. And the scarcity of good conduct, towards those who Allah (swt) loves, is from those matters that bring down Divine Anger. Allah (swt) has declared war against perpetrators of two crimes. The first being interest *(riba)*. Allah (swt) mentions in the Noble Quran:

"O you who believe! Revere God, and leave what remains of usury, if you are believers. And if you do not, then take notice of a war from God and His Messenger..."[10]

As for the second crime, it is harming the righteous friends of Allah (swt) in any way. For the Prophet (s) mentions in a noble *hadith qudsi* that Allah (swt) says: '*I will declare war against him who shows hostility towards a friend of mine...*'[11]

No creation, throughout history has achieved victory in a war against Allah, Most High. Therefore, actions or behaviour that is of little respect to those beloved by Allah (swt), or mocking them, exposes one to severe punishment because of the protective friendship and honour of Allah (swt).

* * *

Imam al-Rabbani (r) says,

"Indeed, one's feeling of self-importance ('ujub) burns good deeds like fire burns wood. Such self-conceit brings about one's admiration for their own deeds. So that one avoids egotism and frees himself from it, one must continually recall shortcomings and defects on the one hand, and on the other, look at one's good deeds as imperfect and deficient. One must also be shy from declaring publicly the good deeds one performed..."

The intention for performing good deeds must be directed only towards reaching the good-pleasure of Allah (swt). The slave must also show gratitude to Allah (swt) for facilitating and giving success in performing the righteous deed. Praising one's self and boastfulness of righteous deeds changes the purpose of those actions and they will not achieve any reward either. This is because there is no space or place for association (*shirk*) in the creed of oneness in Islam *(Aqeedah of Tawheed).*

Based on this, a believer should avoid his name being revealed in connection with any good deed, such as the building of a masjid or school. There is no pressure on one's name being made public in connection with such good deeds after his death by his close ones and such. As that would be a means for his name to be remembered and have prayers sent upon him. But proclaiming one's good deeds during one's life is considered a mistaken action as it harms and corrupts sincerity.

In fact, it is difficult for a slave when he has resolved to perform a good deed – no matter what he expends of effort and care – that he performs it completely pure and free from outer and inner deficiencies.

So, a slave shouldn't exaggerate the importance of any good deed whatever it is and no matter its stature. Rather he should continually recognise his shortcomings and weakness. He should ask Allah (swt) acceptance of it because of His Kindness and Generosity. Also, we should never forget that the matter of righteous deeds is a matter of supplication *(dua)* to Allah (swt) of our need and rests on Allah's (swt) acceptance of it. Hence, the state of the heart on performing good deeds for Allah (swt) carries a critical importance with the knowers of Allah (swt) (*arifeen*) – an importance on par with performing the deed itself. It is necessary that righteous deeds are made sincerely only for the acceptance of Allah (swt), free from mixing one's intention with even the slightest inclination towards attracting the attention of others for praise or respect. Hence, one should strive their utmost to hide one's good deeds from the eyes of men whenever possible.

To the extent it is narrated in a hadith that one of the seven who will be shaded by Allah (swt) under the shade of His throne on the day in which there will be no shade except its shade – will be the one who gives charity so secretly that his left hand doesn't know how much his right hand spent.

However, giving charity publicly is permissible if there is necessity or for some other benefit like encouraging others to spend. Though extreme care must be taken to protect one's self from boastfulness and arrogance and avoid anything that may affect sincerity.

Furthermore, one should, when performing good deeds, restrain one's self from praising oneself even, so we do not feel elation or pride within ourselves. Together with, of course, restraining ourselves from yearning for the praise and admiration of others. As for the most effective treatment for restraining the ego and quietening the self *(nafs)* in this regard is to not forget one's flaws and hidden faults which we suffer from. Otherwise we would not be able to hold our selves back from haughtiness nor achieve the promised reward for good deeds.

We ask Allah (swt) that He make our intentions and deeds sincere and purely for the His Noble Sake and to acquire His Good-Pleasure. And that He give us success – we who are weak, impotent slaves, through His Kindness and Generosity – in achieving righteous deeds and praiseworthy character which He loves and with which He is pleased with. And that He guides us to the straight path and that He protects all of us from being tested in our religion and from being bankrupt in the hereafter. Ameen.

Footnotes

1. Turkish poet, novelist and playwright. 1904 – 1983.
2. Time spent in useless play while the not paying attention to wonder and opportunities the world has to offer.
3. Quran; 51:56.
4. Quran; 23:1-2.
5. Quran: 79:46
6. Bukhari, Adab 96.
7. A term used by some Sufi Tariqas. A simple definition would be that one is so enamoured and in love with the Beloved, that one entirely forgets one's own desires and wishes and sees only those of the Beloved. With the Beloved usually referring to Allah (swt), but sometimes also the Messenger (s) or one's shaykh in the spiritual path. (Depending on the sufi's spiritual level).
8. The story of *Majnoon's* love for *Leila* is akin to Romeo's and Juliet's in English Literature. With Majnoon literally meaning mad-man, an apt description of the crazy depths love can make one fall to.
9. Riyad as-Saliheen 1725
10. Quran; 2:278-279

11. Riyad as-Saliheen 95

CHAPTER 6

Wisdoms from Imam Rabbani - Part 5

The purpose of tassawuf (Sufism) is not obtaining spiritual unveilings, working miracles or witnessing unknown realms. These matters are just shadows on the spiritual journey and may pass and be lost at any moment. Rather, the purpose of following the Sufi way is obtaining a heart immersed in love (of Allah), through being in a state of tranquillity and serenity in faith. It is worshipping Allah with consistency and intimacy with the harmony of both the body and the heart and with praiseworthy, adorned and impressive character. All purposes other than these are just whims and desires of insignificant importance that distances the slave from his true purpose.

Imam al-Rabbani (r) says, '*The purpose of the spiritual path (Sufism) is not to uncover hidden images and forms or witness mysterious colours and lights – for this all comes under useless play and amusement – it is just the turning away from the visible lights and images and instead hankering after the hidden lights and images through self-exertion and practice. Truly those images and colours and these images and colours – all are creations of Allah (swt). All are signs pointing to His existence.*'

The story of *Ba'lan bin Ba'ura* is an example expressing this reality and is mentioned in the Quran.[1] This person was not able to spare himself from Divine Anger and Dominance despite being given many spiritual unveilings and miracles *(karamaat)* because of his inclination towards the world and his allowing himself to being overpowered by his lowly desires.

Extraordinary states like spiritual unveiling *(kashf)* and miracles *(karamaat)* are given to some servants sometimes as a divine kindness and sometimes as a divine test. They are only phases that must be crossed to reach their other sides. Busying one's self with these phases or desiring to remain in them only distances one away from the true journey and primary purpose.

Hence, the righteous do not pay attention to worldly miracles and rather focus their efforts to preserve their steadfastness in religion – which is the true miracle.

It has been narrated that *Abu Yazid al-Bistami (r)* said: '*I arrived once at the Tigris River and wanted to cross to the other bank. Suddenly the two edges of the Tigris joined together so I could pass. So, I said: By Allah, I am not deceived by this! For peo-*

ple cross the Tigris for half a dirham. I am not going to lose the rewards of my life (that is righteous deeds he had prepared for 30 years with the Day of Judgement in mind) for the sake of half a dirham! I want the Glorious One (i.e. Allah), not glory (itself).'

The important matter a slave of Allah (swt) should concern themselves with is moving with sincerity and humility on the path that attains the good-pleasure of Allah (swt). And not be deceived by illusions and deceptive shadows that appear on this path.

Furthermore, obtaining spiritual unveiling *(kashf)* or miracles (or not attaining them) is not the only yardstick to measure spiritual advancement. For example, there are not many narrations that mention the miracles of *Abu Bakr as Siddeeq* (r) and he was the best of mankind after the Prophets and Messengers (a) as is mentioned in many hadith. The greatest miracle of *Abu Bakr* (r) was his belief and unparalleled sincerity and devotion to the Messenger (s) of Allah (swt), as well as his submission and exceptional obedience to him. It (his miracle) is the abundance of the qualities and characteristics of the Prophet (s) in his own self and to the highest degree.

From this it becomes clear that reaching perfection on the spiritual path without passing through spiritual unveilings *(kashf)* and miracles is better and more sound. Those that experience such states are more likely to fall victim to arrogance and vanity because of basic human nature. They are also more inclined to fall into the error of reducing their eagerness to perform good deeds, lessening their efforts in worship and spirituality because of their belief that they have already arrived at a level of perfection and hence there doesn't remain a need for them to exert greater effort or zeal.

All the while, Allah (swt) has commanded in his noble book on the necessity of striving hard in worship until the last breath with His words:

"**And worship your Lord, till there comes the certainty (i.e. death)**"[2]

As for those who continue with patience on the path with steadfastness without witnessing such extraordinary states, they are more cautious and on guard against vanity and arrogance. They look at themselves as continually being deficient. They greatly desire to increase their spiritual efforts and resolve to perform good deeds and to stand before Allah (swt) with complete humility and a with a sense of being nothingness. Taha Al-Hariri points to this reality with his words:

'Truly the state of a seeker of Allah (swt) who has spiritual unveilings (kashf) and one who doesn't is like two travellers journeying to Mecca – one of them can see, the other blind. Both travellers dwell closer to their destination throughout their journey. Except that the blind one has greater and more supreme reward. The same is the situation on the spiritual path and journey. The seeker who is hidden from spiritual unveiling has greater reward – because he is in a state of continual progression.'

Abu al-Hasan al-Khirkani (r) also advised one of his disciples with service of others (*khidma*) for the purpose of reaching spiritual perfection with his words:

'The greatest miracle is being in the service of the creations of Allah, Most High, without weariness or boredom'.

Imam al-Rabbani (r) says,

'After arriving at the two wings of belief and action, by the support of Allah (swt), one should proceed on the high path of tassawuf (of the people taqwa). Not to lean towards another objective other than belief and action, as that would, in the long term, lead one down a slippery slope into error.

The purpose is to arrive at certainty and repose in belief that doesn't fade away on contact with the doubts of the sceptic nor is it dulled by the reference to a momentary doubt.'

The purpose of following the Sufi way is obtaining a heart immersed in love (of Allah), through being in a state of tranquillity and serenity in faith. It is worshipping Allah (swt) with consistency and intimacy with the harmony of both the body and the heart and with praiseworthy, adorned and impressive character. And it is striving to reach the state of being a servant to Allah (swt) with which He is pleased. All purposes other than these are just whims and desires of insignificant importance that distance the slave from his true purpose.

On the other hand, the condition of the believers who are blessed enough to obtain a portion of *tassawuf* training to a greater degree, they can more soundly preserve their faith in the face of oppression, pressures and assaults (to their faith) – that is a historical fact.

It can be noticed that most of those who succeeded in preserving their Islamic identity in Islamic societies around the world, who for years faced operations from communist and atheist regimes on the one hand and intensive missionary operations on the other, were those who benefited from *tassawuf* teachings. This can particularly be seen in the Balkans, Caucuses, Anatolia (Turkey and surrounding regions) and Africa. That is because the purpose of *tassawuf* is strengthening faith (*imaan*) in hearts so that they are resilient against the onslaughts of the most dangerous storms of disbelief *(kufr)* and atheism – without being the slightest bit affected or shaken.

Imam al-Rabbani (r) says:

'The advice which I advise my companions and will continue to advise them with until the end of my life is that after correcting one's belief (aqeedah) in accordance to the books of kalam particular to Ahlus Sunnah wal-Jama'ah[3] - gratitude is to Allah (swt) for their efforts – and after coming to the rules of Fiqh and learning the compulsory (fard), necessary (wajib), advocated (sunnah), recommended (mandoob), the permissible (halal), forbidden (haram), disliked (makruh) and the suspicious (mustabih) – observing by them – after this is arriving at the peace of mind that your heart be connected with none other than Allah (swt)'(i.e. tassawuf).

The matter that the people of truth agree on most is steadfastness on servitude to Allah (swt). To the extent that steadfastness has been termed the greatest miracle (of a friend of Allah). As for the foundation of steadfastness it is first correcting one's beliefs to be in accordance with the standard and balance of the Quran and Sunnah. Then, it is avoiding the forbidden and doubtful and adorning oneself with praiseworthy character, all the while being consistent on righteous deeds.

Our ability to acquire a sound heart *(qalb saleem)* which Allah (swt) wants from us – being in His presence with a heart clean and purified from impurities and defilement – is connected with our performing our external and internal duties and roles with sincerity. We must exert our utmost efforts in this matter so that our hearts are not inclined to anyone other than Allah (when performing our good deeds) and that tranquillity and peace is achieved with the remembrance of Allah (swt).

Let us wholly contemplate the words of Allah (swt):

'We did indeed create man, and We know what his soul whispers to him; and We are nearer to him than his jugular vein.'[4]

Truly, everything that occurs to our minds is hidden and secretive except to Allah (swt) to whom only all things are known and evident. So, this short life should be spent considering this reality. We should make our feelings and thoughts harmonious with the good pleasure of Allah (swt) including our internal states and external actions. And we should distance our hearts from being absorbed by other goals other than Him (swt).

* * *

Imam Rabbani (r) says:

'I do not do any good deed except that I suspect myself about it. Rather I do not relax nor is my heart settled until I suspect myself and look at it as if the good deed is not worthy to be written by the angel of the right (shoulder). And I believe that my right page (of good deeds) is empty of good deeds – its writing having been suspended. Then how can I be deserving to be accepted by Allah (swt)? And I know that everyone in the world from the disbeliev-

ers from amongst the Europeans, to the apostates and atheists are better than me in many respects, and the worst of the lot am I.'

When a person's moral and spiritual level increases, then the feelings of humility and reverence to Allah (swt) also increase. The prophets (a) and *awliya* (r), who are considered to be at the highest level in terms of knowledge of Allah (swt), would beseech Allah (swt), seeking refuge in Him, being aware of their own weaknesses and being humble to a greater degree than most sinners who perpetrate sins. Their eyes flow with tears of regret over their apprehension of their shortcomings (regarding the Majesty of Allah) and they seek His forgiveness and turn to him in penitence.

Our master, *Ibrahim* (a) was faced with trials of sacrifice in the way of Allah (swt) – with his wealth, his self and his children. He had dislodged the temporal loves from his heart. He manifested a difficult, bitter, monotheistic struggle against his pagan people. So, he became the friend of Allah (swt) due to his love, submission and sincerity and reached to the level of being from the people of Allah (swt). Despite his reaching this high level with Allah (swt), he would invoke Allah (swt) with intensive fear, weakness and humility, he said:

'(My Lord...) And disgrace me not on the Day they are resurrected'[5]

No doubt, that this level of fear, terror and humility that is observed amongst the prophets and saints and righteous believers is a sign of their closeness to Allah (swt) and the high levels they have traversed in the knowledge of Allah (swt).

Allah (swt) says in the blessed verse:

'[Yet] only those among His servants who know, fear Allah'[6]

What is intended by knowledge in this verse is knowledge of Allah (swt). A high and elevated understanding of the Greatness and Powers of Allah (swt) and contrarily the weakness of one's self. This is *ma'rifa-tul Allah*[7] (knowledge of Allah).

Allah (swt) clarifies the condition of these righteous slaves who worship Him, together with their sentiments of humility and fear in His Noble Book with the verses:

'...**and those who give what they give while their hearts quake with fear that they shall return to their Lord – it is they who hasten toward good deeds and are foremost in them.**'[8]

The mother of the believers, A'isha (r) says:

'I asked the Messenger (s) of Allah (swt) about this ayah: "Are they those who drink alcohol and steal? (and hence turn repentant to Allah)" He said: "No, O daughter of As-Siddiq. They are those who fast, perform prayer, give charity while they fear that their Lord will not accept it from them: It is these who hasten to do good deeds, and they are the foremost of them.'

It is because of this that anxiety overpowers the hearts of the *awliya*, the righteous and knowers of Allah that they beseech and invoke Allah with the words: *'Praise be to you! We have not been able to know You by Your rightful Worthiness. Nor have we worshipped You as You deserve.'*

Despite the heedless, who may not feel the least God-fear from the greatest of sins they commit, the knowers of Allah (swt) live in state of great anxiety, fear and apprehension on whether their righteous deeds would be accepted or not. This is the state of their awe of Allah (swt), to which Divine Power and Greatness manifested by guiding them towards it.

Imam Ali (r) had said: *'Don't pay attention to the number of deeds but whether they are accepted or not.'*

That is to say that a matter is not completed after performing a righteous deed. Attentiveness should also be given to one's level of sincerity in performing it. And displaying great care to avoid every negative trait which invalidates the reward of good deeds such as showing-off, boasting, conceit, arrogance and other than these.

One of the most important goals of *tassawuf* is, then, the acquirement of hearts that have these subtle feelings and sensitivities combined with a balance of fear and hope.

That is why the 'people of truth' see themselves as being of the lowest of levels, despite their elevation to the stars in the heavens of spirituality. With this, they are conscious of falling into the heedlessness of depending and trusting on their virtuous deeds and spiritual states. Rather, they are distinguished by their contemplating Allah's (swt) Forgiveness and Mercy as the sole reason for their reaching eternal success in Paradise.

Imam al-Rabbani (r) would request from his students in his Letters, which he sent to them, to pray for a good ending. That is that they take their last breaths in this world while having strong and sound faith (*imaan*). The Imam mentioned in one letter which he sent to his son:

'Have mercy on the young and awaken their desire for the recitation of the Quran, fulfill the rights of those under our responsibility whenever possible and support one another in asking for sound faith...'

This inner sensitivity, regarding one's last breaths being with sound and firm faith and having the demeanour of servitude is a re-occurring characteristic of the people of Allah (swt). It is incumbent on all that we take this sensibility of faith as an example and guide.

From this we can see we should never slacken from repeating the prayer which appears in the blessed verse:

'**...Make me die a Muslim and make me join the righteous.**'

That is because no one has the guarantee of leaving this world with faith except the Prophets (a) and those who they gave direct glad tidings to.

We mention in the below incident a truth expressing this reality:

When *Abu Bakr al-Warraq* (r) passed away – and he is considered one of the people of Allah (swt) – one of the righteous saw him in a dream. *Abu Bakr al-Warraq* (r) was pale and crying with grief.

The man asked, 'What is this state O Abu Bakr? Are things good or not!?'

Abu Bakr (r) replied, '*What good? They came with 10 funerals and there wasn't one Muslim amongst them!*'

We ask our Guardian and Protector (swt) that He honour us with a good ending. That He join us, through His Generosity and Kindness, with the exclusive group of His joyous, righteous servants. Those who spent their lives in the struggle to achieve Divine Good Pleasure, and acquired in the last spark of this life, the bliss and joy of the eternal reunion (with Allah) – Ameen!

Footnotes

1. See Quran; [7:175-176]
2. Quran; [15:99]
3. Literally the people of the Prophet's Sunnah and Community
4. Quran; [50:16]
5. Quran; [26:87]
6. Quran; [35:28]
7. Imam Ghazali (r) highlights in his *Ihya Ulum al-*Din in the first chapter, the Book of Knowledge, that *ma'rifa-tul Allah* or knowledge of Allah, is the most important, fundamental and of highest priority knowledge that one must learn.

CHAPTER 7

Wisdoms from Imam Rabbani - Part 6

One day, a death shroud will wrap itself around each and every one of us. It is the final garment in this temporal market of life. Soon death will close and cancel all deals and transactions as well as every temporal desire and lust and deceiving pleasure!

And it will not be possible from that moment onwards, to prepare any deed for the morrow and neither will the regret of the regretful be of any benefit. Hence the day for preparing our accounts so that they profit us with success in the gathering of the Last Day – it is this day, today, now, which we are living...

Imam al-Rabbani (r) says,
'*La ilaha ilal Allah (There is no God but Allah) – nothing is more beneficial than this pure declaration in easing the Anger*

of Allah, His Authority be Majestic, and His proofs be elevated. So, if this declaration is a reason of easing the Anger which takes one into the fire, it is also a reason for easing other punishments, in a similar vein. And how can it not be so, when the servant has turned away from everything other than Him, denying all else by repeating this blessed statement, and made for himself one purpose – the true Deity – while the source of punishment is directing one's self to many various purposes to which the servant has become attracted and afflicted by.'

Amongst the greatest sins that incite and lead to the Anger of Allah (swt) and distances one from divine Mercy are *kufr* (disbelief), *shirk* (polytheism) and *inkaar* (denial) – denial of the existence of God (swt) or placing a partner with Him or denying Him deep down in one's heart even if one appears to be a believer superficially.

Amongst the main reasons for corruptions in man's *fitra* (primordial nature) – which was created so that he would worship Allah (swt) on the way of truth – and the reasons for man's travelling down roads of falsehood are following one's *nafs* (egocentric self) or *shaytan* (satan), or human devils and bringing about one's own destruction. As for what veils man's reason and deadens his heart in this regard, it is, most of the time, due to chasing the different interests and benefits that appear before him that are, in reality, a test and trial.

The following parable of *Fareed ud-deen Al-Attar*[1] (r) carries a great lesson in this matter:

'There was once a sultan who had a skilled hunting dog which he loved dearly. The sultan would give much importance

to this dog and admire it greatly. He would never leave on a hunting expedition except he would bring it with him. It even had a collar encrusted with jewels and anklets of gold and silver on its legs while its back was covered with a garment of woven silk.

One day, the king proceeded on a hunting trip with the men from his fort and took with him this hunting dog as was his custom. The king was fully composed riding on his horse with dignity and in his hand was a silken leash tied to the dog's collar. Suddenly, something happened that ruined the king's trance of euphoria and delight. The dog had suddenly occupied itself with something other than the king – as if it had forgotten him completely. The sultan tried with great force to pull back the leash so that the dog might be dissuaded from what it was occupied with. But alas, the king was only grieved further since his efforts were unsuccessful. The dog continued licking the bone that was in front of it and tried biting it. The sultan was compelled to shout out angrily and with astonishment:

'How can there be such complete distraction in my presence and such forgetfulness of me!?'

The sultan was greatly grieved and bothered. For the denial of him the dog showed and the absence of its loyalty and its heedlessness of him had affected him. The king did not excuse or forgive just because it was a dog. For the dog's busying itself, after the great goodness it had received as well as all the honour and consideration, all of a sudden with a bone and its complete forgetfulness of the king – was not worthy of being forgiven.

The king definitively said, 'Leave to be free this ungrateful, bad-mannered one!'

Once the heedless dog understood the severity and seriousness of the situation, the matter was already done and dusted. Nothing could further be done.

The men said to the sultan, 'O our master. Let us strip away from it the encrusted jewels and the gold and silver. And then let it go!'

The king replied, 'No. Leave it and let it go as it is', before adding by saying, 'let it wander about a stranger, suffering from hunger and thirst in the heat and barrenness of the desert. Then let it look at those jewels, so it lives with the burning thoughts, pain and regret over the blessings and goodness which it lost in front of its very eyes!'

Likewise – and to Allah (swt) belongs the incomparable similitude – what mostly leads to the Anger of Allah (swt), is the attachment of the hearts of men with the creation and turning away from the Creator. The fact is, however, that humans were created for the purpose of worshipping Allah (swt), the Most High, and all creation is only from amongst His creations, and hence, from amongst His blessings upon us.

Hence, there cannot be denial and ingratitude greater than forgetting one's Creator and True King and Sustainer – and then considering seeking assistance from other than Him!

It need not be mentioned that if all humankind denied the Creator (swt), it wouldn't decrease His Majesty not even the weight of an atom. The opposite is also true. If all humankind believed in His Existence and His Unity, it wouldn't increase

His Majesty in the slightest. For Allah (swt) is above any need of our servitude and He is far above any need. Rather belief or denial only benefit or harm one's self.

But besides that, Allah (swt), in accordance with His vast Mercy, desires for humankind guidance and happiness. That they reach the honour of having faith and that they be deserving of His Favour and rewards.

The declaration of *tawheed* (*shahada* or statement declaring God's Oneness) is amongst the most beloved phrases to Allah (swt) as it is a declaration that testifies that there is no other god except Allah.

Understanding this declaration properly and believing in it wholeheartedly requires:

- That the servant turns his face away from all sin and immorality and all temporal, worldly doors, seeking only the divine doorstep of Allah (swt).
- Denial and rejection of all false gods, that are in reality just figments of imagination and whims, and turning towards the one, true and only God.
- Removal and stripping down from one's self all egotistical and satanic connections, that become worshipped idols in our hearts. One would thus be able to achieve true freedom by becoming a real servant to Allah (swt) alone.

Allah (swt) has shown many from amongst mankind His Mercy and Forgiveness on merely their mentioning of the declaration of *tawheed*, even if they were deserving of punishment and discipline. Even the Prophet (s) forgave pagan disbelievers of his time after their mentioning the declaration of tawheed and presenting their regret before him, entering them amongst his companions. This is after the Prophet (s) suffered for many long years under their tyranny.

For instance *Wahshi* (r), who before his Islam killed *Hamza* (r), the uncle of the Prophet (s), later, understanding the reality of the declaration of *tawheed*, set forth, armed with the zeal of faith, to finish off the imposter, *Musailmah* the Liar, who pretended to be a prophet. He did this by way of expiation for his prior sins and to lessen his inner turmoil and burning regret which plagued his heart. In the end, he became a blessed companion who until the end of time will be remembered amongst the believers as Wahshi – *Radi Allahu Anhu* (May Allah be pleased with him) – until the Day of Judgement.

The best means a believer can take to seek forgiveness for themselves is to say the declaration of *tawheed – la ilaha ilaAllah – there is no god but Allah*. This blessed sentence is found in many prayers of repentance and seeking forgiveness.

Certainly, the prayer of our Master Younus (Jonah – upon him be peace) was accepted through his usage of this declaration. It is mentioned in the Noble Quran:

'And [remember] Dhu'l-Nūn, when he went away in anger, and thought We had no power over him. Then he cried out in the darkness, "There is no god but Thee! Glory be to Thee! Truly I have been among the wrongdoers." So,

We answered him, and saved him from grief. Thus, do We save the believers.'[2]

(This incident occurred when Prophet Younes (a) was ordered to call his people to faith and to remain with them for 40 days. However, he left them on the 37th day after losing hope since they were so insistent on disbelief.)

Imam al-Rabbani (r) says:

'The virtue of la ilaha ilaAllah is so great that the entire world is as if nothing when compared with it, not even like a drop compared to a surrounding sea! And the greatness of this pure statement is in accordance with its speaker. Every time the speaker's (spiritual) level increases and rises so too does the greatness of this statement increase.'

The following prophetic hadith clarifies the value and importance of the declaration of tawheed with Allah (swt) as well as its exceptional effect in bringing near divine forgiveness. The companion *Shaddad ibn Aws (r)* narrates:

We were with the Prophet (s) and he said, "Is there amongst you a stranger?" – and he meant anyone from the people of the book[3]. *We said no O Messenger of Allah. The Prophet (s) then ordered the closing of the door and said, "Raise your hands and say: la ilaha ilaAllah!" So we raised our hands for just a moment and the Prophet (s) put down his hands and said, "Praise be to Allah! My Lord, You sent me with this declaration and You ordered me to keep to it and You promised Paradise for it. Truly, You do not break Your promise!" Then he said, "Rejoice! For indeed Allah, be He Glorified and Majestic, has forgiven you all."*

The following incident also expounds the great value and importance of this declaration of *tawheed* with Allah (swt):

Our Master *Suleiman* (Prophet Solomon – upon our Prophet and upon him be peace) was blessed by Allah (swt) with a great kingdom and He subjected to him many things and creatures. One day he was inspecting his great army, composed of jinn, humans and birds. He passed by a valley which was inhabited by many ants and when one of the leaders of the ants saw *Suleiman* (a) and his army approaching she said to her fellow ants, **'O ants! Enter your dwellings, lest Suleiman and his hosts crush you, while they are unaware.**[4] *This is Suleiman, the owner of the great kingdom who has no peer!'*

When *Suleiman* (a) heard her talk – and Allah (swt) had taught him the speech of animals, he said, *'Far from it! My kingdom is but short-lived. As for the kingdom and bliss which the declaration of tawheed brings – that is everlasting forever!'*

It is also mentioned in the honourable prophetic *hadith*, 'He whose last words are la ilaha ilalAllah, shall enter Paradise.'

So, until one attains this prophetic, glad tiding, and reaches the kingdom of eternal happiness, one must exert their utmost effort and striving so that their lives are in accordance with the essence and meaning of the declaration of *tawheed* until their last breath. If the servant can turn away from all other false gods other than Allah (swt) – those that are external and those that are within our own selves, and fill one's heart with faith and live one's life upon this way until the last breath – then it is hoped that one may utter the declaration with his soul in a state of faith and reach eternal Paradise. On the other hand, with few exceptions, it is very difficult for one to live their life contrary to the reality of *la ilaha ilaAllah* and yet be able to utter it at the time of death. As it also comes in another prophetic *hadith*:

"As you live you will die. As you die, you will be resurrected."

Abeedullah Ahrar (r) says:

After Shaykh Shah Naqshaband passed away, one of the awliya (saints) saw him in a dream and asked him, 'What should we do in order to reach eternal success?

The Shaykh replied, 'Busy yourself with what you should be busy with at the time of the last breath!' That is to say, just as one knows it to be necessary to busy one's self with thoughts of Allah (swt) alone during the agonies of death, so be like that, be alert and pondering about Allah (swt) throughout your life!

Man should be busy with preparing himself for the goal of having faith at that moment of separation from this life, with consistency and enduringly. To think that eternal success can be achieved with just uttering empty words even if it is the declaration of *tawheed*, without living under the shade and in the essence of those words – then that is like chasing a deceiving mirage.

Imam Zuhri (r), who was one of the great scholars from the generation of the *tabieen*,[5] was asked about the hadith: "*Whoever says la ilaha ilaAllah will enter Paradise*". The Imam said about it, '*This was regarding the time at the beginning of Islam, before the enjoining of duties (fara'id) and before the commands and prohibitions.*'[6]

It is necessary, in order to arrive at complete religion, to observe the rules and judgements that appear in the Quran and Sunnah and to live under the shade of the declaration of *tawheed*. Allah (swt) has clarified in His Noble Book, the irrationality of thinking that eternal salvation is achieved by merely speaking a few words without living by them:

'Does mankind suppose that they will be left to say, "We believe," and that they will not be tried?'[7]

It has also been narrated that this noble verse was revealed concerning some of the noble companions who were faced with various tyrannies, punishments and oppressions on account of their faith. These narrations make clear that true faith has a price that needs to be paid. The Noble Quran informs us of the story of the magicians at the time of Pharaoh who sacrificed their lives in way of saving their faith, the story of the people of the trench who were thrown into pits of fire because of their refusing to give up their faith and the story of *Habib al-Najjar* who was martyred with stones as he protected the religion of the One God.

Besides this, Imam al-Rabbani (r) mentions that the value and magnitude of the declaration of *tawheed* in the divine scales is in accordance with the spiritual rank of the speaker. Hence, the importance of delving deeply into the meaning of the declaration of *tawheed* and understanding its realities. As for the spiritual rank of the noble companions, Abdullah ibn Masood (r), who himself spiritually excelled to advanced levels under the tutelage of the Prophet (s) would express it with his saying: '*We would hear the praising of Allah from the food we would be eating.*'

* * *

Imam Rabbani (r) says:

What is intended from saying – la ilaha ilaAllah – is doing away with all false gods. Both those that are deemed to be external and are different entities as well as those inside of us. The external ones are the gods of the disbelievers and polytheists, like Laat and Uzza[8]. *As for the internal gods they are desires and lusts of the human self. Allah (swt) says:* **'Have you considered one who takes his desires as his god...?'**[9] *The obligations of the shariah as well as belief in one's heart are enough to rid of external gods. As for removal of those false inner gods, purification (tazkiya) of the evil-commanding self is required (nafs al-ammara).*

This matter is the purpose and result of travelling on the way of the 'people of Allah'. Arriving at true faith is linked to ridding one's self of these two classes of false gods.'

The declaration of *tawheed*, begins with the words *la ilaha...* (there are no gods) – that is, denial and turning away from all the false gods. Confirming to faith by following the *Shariah* and believing in Allah as the One God are enough in denying all the false gods of the disbelievers, polytheists, false deities and such. But this is perhaps the easier part of arriving to the truth of God's oneness *(tawheed)*. As for the more difficult part, it is the crushing of the hidden idols and deities in the inner world of man and being able to solely submit to Allah (swt), alone.

This is the meaning and wisdom of the Prophet's (s) saying when he returned from the battle of *Tabuk* – a great and difficult battle: '*We have returned from the smaller jihad to the greater jihad.*'

They asked, "What is the greater jihad?

He replied, 'The struggling of the servant against his desires.'

That is why the cleansing of the egotistical self and the purification and decontamination of our inner world from false gods is a very difficult affair, and of higher priority and more of a necessity.

It is mentioned in the Noble Quran:

'Successful indeed are those who purify themselves, remember the Name of their Lord, and pray.'[10]

Ibn Abbas (r) explains the word *tazakka* (literally from the root word: to purify) in this noble verse with the saying '*la ilaha ilalAllah*'. Because, the first step in the way of (spiritual) purification is cleansing the heart from disbelief and the propping up of partners with Allah (*shirk*).

So then, what are these idols in our inner worlds that we require to be cleansed from? They include:

- The desires and lusts of the self which occupy greater importance for the servant than fulfilling the commands of Allah (swt).
- All temporal benefits that the servant should renounce in travelling the path to Allah (swt), yet he re-

fuses to do so. Preferring the passing worldly life over the eternal hereafter when there is a clash between them.
- Desire for rank or status – a position that keeps the servant distant from Allah (swt).
- Fame and riches that cause the servant to forget his Creator (swt).

Allah (swt) has empowered the forbidden things of this world with great alluring power as a divine test for us. The shield against these attractions requires great faith and determination.

The polytheists of Mecca once came to the Prophet (s) and requested that he end his ideological attack on their idols with the following proposition which they offered:

'If what you desire by spreading this message is wealth, we will gather for you from amongst our own wealth until you be the richest amongst us! If you desire honour, we shall make you our leader, that we will not decide on any matter without you! If you desire kingdom, we will make you a king over us! If you want women, we shall marry you to the most beautiful women of the Arabs!'

This is how the noble Prophet (s) rejected them:

'What concern do I have over what you mention? I haven't come to you all with what I have, to ask for your money or the honour amongst yourselves nor kingdom over you. Except Allah has sent me to you as a messenger and revealed upon me a book and commanded that I be to you a bearer of glad tidings (with

knowledge of God and of Paradise) and a warner (of Hellfire if you reject). So, I conveyed to you the messages from my Lord and advised you. If you accept what I bring to you, that is your good fortune in this world and the next. If you reject me, then I patiently wait for the command of Allah until He judges between yourselves and I.'

No doubt, that such offers and temptations didn't affect the Prophet (s), not even the amount of an atom. He who was sent with the mission of abolishing the external gods and purifying inner selves from inner gods. Human history is filled with uncountable numbers of people who were deceived or had weak willpower and answered the call of this world for the sake of their desires and forgot the Hereafter, becoming immersed with their temporal desires and lusts.

It is mentioned in a prophetic *hadith*:

'*I don't fear that you take up partners with Allah (commit the external shirk), however I fear the (temptations of the) world and that you compete in them.*'

Summing up, the greatest false god, that man actually worships, while forgetting his true Master and Creator, is his own self *(nafs)*. From it come overpowering decisions that prevent the orders of Allah (swt) from being implemented. It is the saying "in my opinion..." when it contradicts and challenges the divine realities. It is personal, impulsive judgements that don't concur with the rules of Islam. It is not performing the practices of Islam with the intention of fulfilling the commands of Allah (swt) but rather with intentions mixed with lowly, worldly goals and purposes, like seeking stature among people, or not wanting to lose importance or status among them – that is preforming the practices for showing off not for the good-pleasure of one's Lord (swt).

It is mentioned in the Noble Quran:

'Have you seen (O Prophet) the one who has taken their own desires as their god? Will you then be a keeper over them?'

And it is mentioned in a Prophetic *Hadith*:

'There is not under the shade of the heavens a god that is worshipped alongside Allah greater than followed desires.'

Based on what was just mentioned, the purification of the self *(nafs)* with training, spirituality and cleansing it from impurities and filth is of the utmost importance and necessity. One cannot arrive at the reality of the declaration of *tawheed* except through removing these inner partners put up besides Allah (swt).

We ask Allah, our Guardian that He give all of us success in mentioning the declaration of *tawheed* its rightful mention. And that He make easy our grasping and understanding of the realities of it, and that He make our whole lives with all of its states, actions and words in accordance with the standard and balance of *tawheed* and that He bestows upon us the safety of *imaan* (belief) and a good ending at the time of death.

Ameen!

Footnotes

1. 13th century Persian saint and poet. Author of The Conference of the Birds.
2. Quran; 21:87-88
3. People of the Book, i.e. Jews or Christians.
4. Quran; 27:18
5. Generation of pious believers that lived after the companions of the Prophet (s).
6. Tirmidhi; Al-Imaan; 17-2638 (Arabic Reference)
7. Quran; 29:2
8. Pagan idols worshipped in Arabia by the polytheists before being eradicated by Islam.
9. Quran; 45:23.
10. Quran; 87:14.

CHAPTER 8

Wisdoms from Imam Rabbani - Part 7

Every gathering filled with spiritual radiance is fundamentally a breeze of mercy that has reached our time from the gatherings of the Messenger of Allah (swt) and from the age of bliss (i.e. from the time of the Prophet (s)). Just as candles are lit by other candles, and the flame, which lights the candle and illuminates its surroundings, is the same flame itself...if the believer is illuminated by even the last of these candles it is as if he derived the light from its original source...

Imam al-Rabbani (r) says,
'The time now is the time of remembrance (dhikr), so put your selfish inner desires under the scope of the 'la' in the declaration of tawheed (i.e. include it in la ilaha ilalAllah) until they are fully non-existent and there doesn't remain any selfish or egotistical purpose or goal in your chest...

In regard to the second part of the declaration, i.e. the affirmation 'ilaAllah' (except Allah), there should be nothing else or meant in our hearts other than the secret of the Oneness of Allah (swt) – who is the source behind all real things and imaginings – such as homes, palaces, wells, gardens, books and others - and He facilitates all of them. Don't let anything else crowd up your time and thoughts!'

That is to say, removal and erasure of all idols and deities, worldly desires and selfish egotism from the heart with the proclamation of *'la'* (no god) in the declaration of *tawheed*, and substitution of that with the love of Allah (swt) alone in the heart with the proclamation of *'ila Allah'* (except Allah). There should never be in the heart any love that conflicts with the love of Allah (swt). Especially, egotism and worldly purposes and goals should be eliminated.

It is mentioned in the noble prophetic hadith:

*'La ilaha ilaAllah will continue to ease the discontent of Allah against His slaves (because of their sins and deficiencies) except if, they are in a state in which they return home not caring about their weakness in religion as long as they are assured in their worldly matters. Were they then to say 'la ilaha ilaAllah', Allah (swt) replies to them: **You have lied.**'*[1]

The creed of *tawheed* (God's Oneness) does not tolerate any partner (with Allah) in any manner, shape or form. Just as the Muslim who is considered from the people of tawheed, rejects all false gods in the outer world and believes in his Lord (swt) alone with no partners attributed to him, the Muslim must also abide by the meaning and spirit of tawheed when remembering Allah *(dhikr)* which is the most personal meeting with Allah (swt) as well as throughout all other practices of worship. Worldly thoughts and thoughts of the egotistical self shouldn't enter between the slave and Allah (swt). He should also pay great attention to avoid all states and actions that may harm the essence of tawheed.

It is mentioned in another prophetic hadith:

'The most dreaded thing I fear for my nation is placing partners with Allah (shirk). I do not mean that they worship a sun or a moon or an idol. Rather that they act for other than Allah or for hidden desires.'[2]

True sincerity – to worship wholly for Allah (swt) alone – cannot be totally achieved except by way of arriving at the truth and reality of *tawheed*. This is one of the main issues that the people of Allah addressed. The late *Najeeb Fadhil* makes mention of this matter in one of his poems in which he depicts the people of truth:

'If any selfish thought flows into their worship, they complete it and repeat it – again and again.

If their eyes waver away (from Allah) to something else for even a moment, then its price is tears till the end of their days.

They desire not Paradise nor salvation from Hellfire, they see only Allah and His Good-Pleasure alone.'

The essence or the reality of the declaration of *tawheed* is cleansing the heart and purifying it from all else other than Allah (swt). After the devotion of the heart to Allah (swt) alone, it begins to have greater sensitivity in the domain of 'knowledge of Allah' (*ma'rifat-ul Allah*) and becomes more susceptible to divine kindnesses and Mercy.

Just as the rays of the sun are bundled and focused at one point when they shine through a magnifying glass, and then burn into ashes what comes before it from grass to wood, likewise every believer should intensify the declaration of *tawheed* in his heart and let it have power over desires and lusts that are gathered in the ego so that it may cleanse and purify it from them.

It has been clarified through the following statement of *Shaykh Esat Erbili*[3], the necessity of exerting much effort to live in accordance with the declaration of *tawheed* in regard to beliefs, acts of worship, transactions with others, behaviour – in short, in regard to every aspect of the life of servanthood. He says:

'*Indeed, this weak brother of yours is still trying to reach perfect faith. And I struggle to remember the declaration of tawheed with my state and with by tongue (through the body and the tongue of the heart). For if there is found in the heart something desired other than Allah then it is extremely difficult to pronounce – la ilaha ilaAllah (in regard to reaching the reality behind the declaration of tawheed). Even if this declaration is repeated superficially, there is doubt if it will be a true means to excel spiritually or be worthy of acceptance.*'

Imam al-Rabbani (r) says:

'*The opportunity is small but spending it on the most important of tasks is necessary, and that is to have the companionship of the masters of the society (accompaniment of the righteous ones). Don't trade this companionship with anything else – whatever it may be. Don't you see that the companions of the Prophet (s) where preferred and honoured above all other people – other than the prophets (a) – through their companionship of the Prophet* (s)'

The first condition from benefitting from companionship – which is one of the most important means of spiritual development and training – is to first understand its importance and value.

Let us first realise that companionship is a prophetic method of training and discipline. For the Prophet (s) nurtured the noble companions and raised them in the best way through his companionship.

The fact that the words companion (*sahabah*) and companionship (*suhbah*) are derived from the same root letters (in Arabic) is a clear and evident indication of this matter. What makes a companion a companion, is their receiving of a portion of the spiritual radiance from the companionship of the Prophet (s), while having true faith and sincerity.

Hence, companionship is considered a stressed action that is to be emulated (*sunnat-ul muakkada*). It is not compulsory or necessary but is a strong *sunnah*[4]. The Prophet (s) was consistent on it and it was rare that he left it – so that it wouldn't become decisively compulsory. The Prophet (s) did not give every companion a book or written notes, rather he gave greater priority to companionship and affinity of hearts.

Companionship is teaching face to face. And together with the Prophet's (s) sayings, his actions and his confirmations, the great effect of his spiritual state which radiated from his smiling visage and illuminating glances – all this had an indescribable effect to those around him. Just as the noble companions benefitted from the blessed sayings of the Prophet (s) in the sphere of close companionship, they also were benefitting from his spiritual states and each companion in accord to his own spiritual readiness and capabilities. As a result of this, the noble companions reached the goal of being adorned of something of the spiritual state of the Prophet (s) in varying degrees in accordance with their aptitudes and predispositions. And their hearts were filled with the spiritual radiances from the Messenger (s) of Allah (swt).

Because of this honour they received, resulting from their companionship of the Prophet (s), none of the righteous ones coming after the companions can reach to their same level, even if they increased in their worship.

Imam al-Rabbani (r) says:

'Indeed, the pivot of benefit of this tariqa (Sufi path) rests on companionship – talking and writing are not sufficient on it'

In spiritual companionship, and likewise in the companionship through speech and knowledge, spiritual radiance flows from heart to heart. This matter is of great importance to the gatherings in congregations – that is the spreading of positive vibes from those present in the congregation from one to another.

Spiritually speaking, in companionship, a spiritual and reciprocal link is established between hearts, like an attractive magnetic field. Sensitivities or feelings flow from this connection and with the passing of time, the qualities of the hearts begin to be similar and so they resemble each other regards to tastes, sympathies, opinions and thoughts.

Certainly, Allah (swt) mentions in His Noble Book:

'O believers! Be mindful of Allah and be with the truthful.'[5]

That is because the acquirement of truthfulness, that is the transformation into a truthful human being is a natural and obvious result from this companionship of hearts.

In fact, (it can be observed that) there is a tendency of all created things to become unified. This particular quality is generated by (and is a sign of) the oneness of the origin of creation. So, for example, if a vial of perfume is diffused in one corner of a room, its fragrance will continue to flow through the air particles that absorb it to others until the fragrance's distribution is the same between all air particles in that room.[6]

This characteristic can be applied over other opposites such as heat and cold, light and darkness – and is a principle effective also in the realm of the heart.

The *Naqshbandi Shaykh Muhammed Al-Khadimi (r)*, one of the great scholars from the Ottoman period said:

'Spiritual states are contagious, to the extent that those states that are present in people that attend gatherings of friendship and companionship flow from one to another...and the natures of people tend to imitate some and follow others. Personalities make impressions on others without people realising so...'

Also, as it appears in the popular proverb - *'There is a path from one heart to another'*.

The important means which increases this transmissibility occurring between hearts – is love. Hence it is important in gatherings of spirituality that there remains in one's heart alertness and continual accepting while the heart has feelings of love, respect and politeness. Meaning, it is not enough to merely have physical closeness – there must also be a closeness and affinity of hearts.

The gatherings of the Messenger of Allah (swt) would proceed with such a harmonious atmosphere. Whenever the Prophet (s) would speak the noble companions would listen to him as if with their entire beings and as if they didn't want a single word to pass them by. This state of conduct, politeness and tranquillity which overpowered them in the gatherings of the Messenger of Allah (swt) is expressed in their saying – *'(we listened to the Prophet) as if there sat birds upon our heads'*.[7]

The following incident is a prominent and eloquent example of how the noble companions benefitted from the gatherings of the Prophet (s).

Thawbaan (r) was the freed slave of the Messenger of Allah (the Messenger (s) had freed him from slavery). Thawbaan did not own anything from the world, except maybe for a single tent. Even so, he came to the Prophet (s) and would be present in his gatherings and would listen to his talks with the most enthusiasm and presence, and it was as if he was progressing from spiritual state to spiritual state through the spiritual delight which he gained from the accompaniment of the Prophet (s).

One day Thawbaan (r) was in the gathering of the Prophet (s) and began to look at the Beloved of Allah (i.e. the Prophet (s)) with deep fixation, when suddenly there appeared on him the signs of anxiety and grief so much so that even his colour changed. His uneasy and saddened state drew the attention of the Prophet (s) – who was sent as mercy to the worlds – the Prophet (s) asked him with compassion and mercy:

"What is the matter, O Thawbaan? What has changed your colour?"

Thawbaan replied, 'O Messenger of Allah! You are more beloved to me than my son, than myself, and more than the entire world. I don't have any sickness or any pain other than when I don't see you, in which case I feel extremely alone and saddened until I meet you. Then I remember the Hereafter and fear that I will not see you if I enter Paradise in the lowest level and you are raised higher than even the Prophets (a) and if I don't enter Paradise, I will never see you again...'

And the glory of all creation (s) was silent for a moment then he replied, *'A person is with the one he loves.'*[8]

And the following Words of Allah (swt) were revealed on this occasion:

'And whoever obeys Allah and the Messenger will be in the company of those blessed by Allah: the prophets, the people of truth, the martyrs, and the righteous—what honourable company!'[9]

All consideration of the noble companions (r) and their striving and exertion was directed towards the continuation of their companionship with the Messenger of Allah (swt) in the

Hereafter, which they were so lucky to receive in this worldly life. And so, they acted to remain in their companionship of the Messenger of Allah (swt) – in its highest meaning and form eternally. And so, they lived with him (s) not only in physical companionship but also with the companionship of spiritual states, and the companionship of similar action, and the companionship of similar sentiments, and the companionship of similar thoughts. And they felt great joy – that defies description – in their obedience to Allah (swt) and His Messenger (s). They were also grateful and eager to sacrifice everything in the path of Allah (swt). The foundations for these spiritual enlightenments were all laid down in the gatherings of companionship.

Likewise, our taking part in spiritual gatherings should be with full presence and eagerness, listening to what is said with the utmost attention and courtesy even if the raised topic is known to us from before. That is because spiritual gatherings are a reminder to he who knows and a teaching to he who doesn't know but more important than that, is the valuable opportunity to benefit from the spiritual radiances from hearts through the companionship of the righteous and truthful ones. We relate in what follows a few incidents which clarify this reality.

Imam Ahmed bin Hanbal (r), one of the great scholars and leaders in knowledge, would visit *Bishr al-Hafi*[10] (r) frequently and say to him,

'*O Bishr! Talk to me about my Lord.*'

Until his students would say to him, '*You are a renowned scholar of hadith and fiqh, and you are qualified to make judgements in many religious fields (ijtihad), we don't see for you an equal in knowledge in your time, yet you frequent a wandering-about madman who doesn't deserve to be even by your side?!*'

The Imam (r) replied, '*In all you have mentioned I may be more knowledgeable than he, but he has more knowledge than me about Allah (swt)*'

Great personalities of knowledge would attend the gatherings of Shaykh Sami Efendi (r) in his time. These scholars, who at times surpassed the shaykh in the external sciences, would sit in his presence with courtesy, humility and great stillness observing total silence and would savour in this climate of spiritual companionship that they couldn't find in their debates among themselves or in between the covers of their books.

From this standpoint, every believer, whether a scholar or ignorant one, needs the spiritual radiance of such spiritual companionship throughout their lives. This need does not ever end! The following incident expounds this fact.

One of the students of *Shaykh Abul Hassan al-Shadhili* (r) had stopped attending his gatherings. One day, the Shaykh came across this student and asked him,

'*Why have you distanced yourself from us and left our gatherings?*'

The student replied, '*I have received sufficient lessons of knowledge from you until now, I don't feel I need to be amongst you anymore.*'

This reply saddened the Shaykh and he said, 'Look my son. If keeping company for a short while is sufficient to receive spiritual blessings and knowledge, Abu Bakr as Siddeeq (r) would have been satisfied with the spiritual radiance and knowledge which he received at the hands of the Prophet (s), except Abu Bakr (r) did not spare a day away from the companionship of the Prophet (s), nor did he part from the Prophet (s), until he returned to his Lord'.

The noble companions (r) were not content with spending long periods of time without seeing the Messenger (s) of Allah (swt), or be absent from his gaze or being deprived from listening to his advices overflowing with wisdom. And they would encourage their children towards such matters. So, see how distant we and our children are from these lofty attitudes of the noble companions. And to what extent do we struggle and endeavour to be in the presence of the righteous and the scholars who are considered to be the inheritors of the Prophet (s), and to benefit from them?

Ismail Hakki al-Buriswi (r) says:

'If the opportunity to be present in the gatherings of the Prophet (s) and companions have passed us, then the possibility of being in the "companionship" of his noble Sunnah and with those that love his Sunnah remains. And so it will remain until the Day of Judgement. Being in the presence of the leaders (in spiritual matters) and closeness with the pious is an overflowing of spiritual radiance.'

And subsequently, the spiritual gatherings in which its proper manners are observed, are a reflection of the gatherings of the Messenger (s) of Allah (swt). For every sitting surrounded by spiritual blessings is, in fact, a merciful breeze that reaches us today from the gatherings of the Messenger (s) of Allah (swt), a euphoria from that age of happiness. Just as candles are lit by other candles, and the flame, which lights the candle and illuminates its surroundings, is the same flame itself...if the believer is illuminated by even the last of these candles he becomes as if he has derived the light from its original source.

Hence, those that attend the gatherings of spiritual intimacy should abide by its etiquettes and honour it greatly as if they were present in one of the circles in which the Prophet (s) himself was present, so that there may flow a spiritual affect into their hearts from that source.

* * *

Imam al-Rabbani (r) says:

'From the obvious is that this world is the place of action not the place of relaxation or idleness. So, you must focus all your efforts towards action! And leave pleasure and comfort and pastimes aside...and leave laziness and sluggishness as a fortune for the enemies! There must be the performance of righteous deeds, then again the performance of righteous deeds, then again the performance of righteous deeds...'

That is the believer, should take advantage of his capital of time in the best manner possible – and that is through understanding the temporality of this world and the limitlessness of the Hereafter. Nor should one forget that the world is as if a harvest that requires difficult toil and great activity and deeds. And the result of this harvest – whether good or bad – shall be reaped in the Hereafter. Basically, the human being who has realised this reality won't allow even a single minute to be wasted in laziness and idleness.

Yet, despite man knowing well all these realities, most of them don't succeed in overpowering their weakness in fulfilling their duties. That is also why, knowledge on its own is not enough, and must be accompanied by sincere action.

Once, *Ibrahim ibn Adham* (r) was asked,

'What is wrong with us, that we call upon Allah, but He doesn't answer us?'

He replied, 'You know Allah, but do not fulfill His rights!

You claim that you love the Messenger (s) of Allah (swt), but you have abandoned his Sunnah!

You read the Quran, but don't act upon it!

You eat the blessings of Allah (swt), but don't offer due gratitude!

You say shaytan is your enemy, yet you don't oppose him!

You say Paradise is true, yet you don't act for it!

You say Hellfire is true, yet you don't flee from it!

You say death is a reality, yet don't prepare for it!

You have buried the corpses of your dead, yet you still have not heeded!

Then how are your prayers to be answered?'

Knowledge alone is not enough and sincere action must accompany it. To wait for a response to our prayers without exerting effort, or to hope for mercy without bearing difficulties, or to wish to receive blessings without striving or facing problems is like someone who wishes to fill his stomach with food that others have already eaten – a useless hope and desire that brings no benefit. Likewise, one cannot reach the rewards of the Hereafter with faith that is without the sacrifices that are necessitated by it in this world.

Hence, it is incumbent on us that we strive with serious effort to perform good deeds which are required by faith before the running out of the blessing of time.

We must aim to spend every moment of our lives with the application of, or the search for, righteous deeds which may be a means for us to reach the Good-Pleasure of Allah (swt). That is the spoken command of Allah:

'So, once you have fulfilled (your duty), strive (in devotion), turning to your Lord (alone) with hope'[11]

We ask Allah, Most High, that He make easy for us all, the spending of our lives in His Good-Pleasure, that He gives us the good news of eternal happiness in our last breaths, and that He honours us, through His Generosity and Kindness, with a life in the Hereafter, filled with tranquillity, being reunited with Him, and admiring His everlasting and inconceivable Beauty...

Ameen.

Footnotes

1. Al-Bayhaqi: Shiab al-Imaan, 100/10015; Al-Haythami: 7/277 (Arabic references)
2. Ibn Majah: Al-Zuhd, 21. (Arabic reference).
3. Sufi Shaykh of Turkey passed away in 1931.
4. Actions of the Prophet (s) that should be emulated. Although there is no punishment for leaving them, hence they are not obligatory, but there is spiritual loss.
5. Quran; 9:119
6. i.e. chemical equilibrium. The property of created things tending towards unification can also be observed through the law of gravity, and the tendency of humans to form families and societies.
7. Abu Dawud; Al-Sunnah: 23-24/4753 (Arabic Reference)
8. Al-Bukhari: Al-Adab,96 (Arabic Reference)
9. Quran; 4:69
10. Literally Bishr the Barefoot. An 8th Century C.E sufi wali. It is said he was a drunkard and one day as he was staggering drunk through the streets of Baghdad, he found a piece of paper on the floor in which the name of Allah (swt) was written. He picked it up, bought

some perfume and perfumed it before placing it in a reverent position in his house. That night he saw a dream in which he heard a voice – '*Thou has perfumed My Name, so I have perfumed thee, thou has exalted My Name, so I have exalted thee. Thou have purified My Name, so I have purified thee. By My Majesty, I will surely perfume thy name in this world and the world to come*'. – Mentioned in Farid ud-Deen Al-Attar's Biography of the saints (*Tazkirat al-Awliya*).

11. Quran; 94:7-8.

www.ingramcontent.com/pod-product-compliance
Lightning Source LLC
Chambersburg PA
CBHW021407290426
44108CB00010B/428